Life Cycle

*A Bike Ride Round Scotland and
Back to Childhood*

Gary Sutherland

BIRLINN

First published in 2013 by
Birlinn Limited
West Newington House
10 Newington Road
Edinburgh
EH9 1QS

www.birlinn.co.uk

ISBN: 978 1 78027 136 1

British Library Cataloguing-in-Publication Data
A catalogue record for this book is available from the British Library

Typeset by Iolaire Typesetting, Newtonmore
Printed and bound by Grafica Veneta
www.graficaveneta.com

For my future wingman Alexander – and Auntie Ishbel,
who taught me how to fly

'Is it about a bicycle?'
The Third Policeman, *Flann O'Brien*

Contents

Acknowledgements

Cheers, min

First of all I'd like to thank my brother Stewart for joining me on an unforgettable bike ride and not bashing into any bollards. We made it back to Dunbar Street, Herb! Secondly I'd like to thank my Auntie Ishbel (aka The Godmother) for sending me on the road to two-wheeled happiness all those years ago, albeit via a bed of nettles. Stewart and I would also like to give a special shout out to cousin Sarah on her beloved Raleigh Budgie.

Huge love and thanks to Clare, Isabella and Alexander; Elaine; Mam; Julieann, John, Blair, Fern and Brogan; Granny and Minnie and everyone who saw us off and welcomed us back. *Merci beaucoup* to Monsieur James Attridge, a vital part of our peloton in the Highlands. Bike hats off (and an advance curlew warning) to Alasdair Fraser who pedalled all the way from Amsterdam to Copenhagen, while we were panting round Scotland, and raised a mighty amount of cash for the Cystic Fibrosis Trust. Well done again, min.

Cheers to Joe at Gear Bikes in Glasgow and heid bike dude Alasdair Maclennan. My brother would also like to thank both Gordon Grant, who did up his Tuff Burner and training buddy Gary Sinclair who, Stewart points out, did far more training than I did. For hospitality on the road, the grateful Sutherland brothers would like to thank Evelyn, Brian Willox, Caroline, John the Chief and Linda, Victor, Jan and Mandi. And for the lowdown on Bamse and the Southside Shuffle, thank you, Jade Smith.

Thanks too to all the hotel, B&B and hostel owners who put us up and fed us and to the hostelries that watered us – especially the Crask Inn and The Anderson!

Still on the topic of beer, we'd like to say cheers to Al and Nige at Windswept Brewing in Lossiemouth for helping make it a legendary homecoming party on Hopeman beach.

Cheers, min, to Steve, Andrew, Dougie, Drew, Mike, Moondo, Mingus, Kev, Marky, Mojo, Lor, Ed, Oog, Mario, Bert and all the other Hopeman heroes. And I still maintain I wouldn't be writing today if it hadn't been for the massive influence Mrs MacIver had on me as a pupil at Hopeman Primary. Bookish gratitude to Neville, Andrew and all at Birlinn, Helen Bleck, Stan, Bob McDevitt, Wayne and everyone at Waterstone's in Elgin. Stewart and I would also like to applaud everyone whose generosity helped us raise a big-hearted £1,400 for Children 1st through our bike ride. And if you fancy cycling some of those roads we travelled, sustrans.org.uk is a good place to start.

Finally, this daft book is for you, Mark and Craig. A good deal of the magic of a Hopeman childhood was down to you pair. Never forgotten, missed as much as ever. I like to picture the two of you having a pint with Captain James. Cheers.

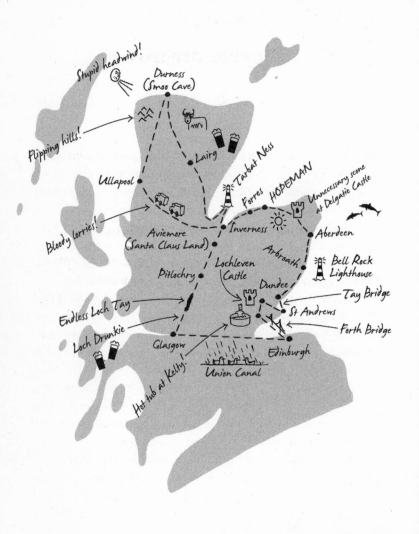

Introduction

Bicycle dreams

The thing about bicycles is you can chart your childhood by them. At least I can. Both the sorest and saddest episodes of my early years are bike-related.

Sorest episode of my childhood

I'm five years old and the stabilisers have been removed from my Raleigh Strika in anticipation of my first solo flight.

We're at the park in Hopeman, me and my Auntie Ishbel, who's lending her godson some vital support as he attempts the biggest feat since he learned to walk. It's a beautiful summer's day and I'm on the cusp of becoming a cyclist. I'm about to experience one of life's great thrills.

My auntie lets go and − look at me! − I'm pedalling away, like some sort of boy genius. This is ace, check me out! I'm in command of a moving vehicle with no stabilisers and the world looks insane from where I'm sitting. What a trip.

But wait a minute, I'm beginning to wobble. My balance isn't quite what it was a moment ago. There's a good chance I might fall. In fact, yes, I am going to fall and it's only going to be one of two ways. To my right is freshly cut summer grass and on my left is a bed of nettles.

Looking back now, I'm wondering why my auntie had me learning to ride my bike beside a bed of nettles. But it's too late because I'm falling into that bed of nettles wearing a T-shirt, shorts and sandals (it's the height of summer, after all).

My bike is on top of me and my limbs feel like they are on fire. My face stings too, like I can't believe. I start crying like the child I am. My auntie reaches down and pulls me out from under my bike.

All I remember after that is sitting on my mam's knee in the kitchen, covered head to toe in calamine lotion.

Then there's the saddest episode of my childhood

I'm over the trauma of the nettles and I'm riding my silver Strika up and down Dunbar Street. I love that bike more than anything, more than my replica Thunderbird 2 (with Thunderbird 4 inside the pod).

My mam calls me in for lunch and I leave my bike at the back gate. Once I've finished my bowl of soup, I run back outside, only to discover that my bike is gone. It's been pinched in broad daylight.

The whole family jumps in the car and we scour the village in the vain hope of catching a thief on a silver Strika. Down to the harbour, over by the beach huts, but there's no sign of it. My beloved bicycle is gone.

That night I cry myself to sleep, and the night after that. This is the worst thing in the world. Even now, three decades later, I can see me sobbing into my pillow while my mam and dad try to comfort me.

Thank goodness some of my happiest childhood memories involve bicycles!

Like the Christmas morning my younger brother Stewart and I got up to find a pair of Raleigh Racers in the living room. Before you could say Rudolf the Red-Nosed Reindeer, we were dressed and out of the house, pedalling the two miles to Duffus beneath a clear blue sky, taking occasional sips of diluted orange juice from our water bottles and pretending we were in the Tour de France.

The unstoppable Sutherland brothers, joy unconfined.

An hour later we were home, worn out but happy and ready to open the rest of our presents.

What it is to get a brand new bike on Christmas Day.

Raleigh ruled our childhoods, as with most kids of our generation.

Between the stolen Strika and the speedy Racer, I was the proud owner of a Grifter XL, a jet-black number with neon flashes, red crash pad on the handlebar and red mudguards. And, best of all, a three-speed gear shift on the right handle grip. That twisting, gear-changing action was the coolest thing. The Grifter XL was the motorbike of bicycles, the dark knight of my dreams.

As futuristic as it looked, it was one heavy beast. Mounting a kerb was a challenge, pulling a wheelie was nigh-on impossible. Even with the luxury of gears, riding a Grifter XL was like riding a bike through soup.

Still, it was utterly indestructible. I must have ridden a million miles on that thing.

Riding alongside me was my wingman, my wee brother Stewart, but he pretty much upstaged me on his Tuff Burner (another Raleigh number, naturally). The Tuff Burner was, quite frankly, the coolest bike that ever existed.

This was a thing of sheer beauty: blue frame wrapped in yellow pads and yellow mag wheels with blue tyres (blue tyres!). Had Willy Wonka been a bike designer rather than a sweetie maker, he would have dreamt up the Tuff Burner. It was the mad-capped mother of BMXs.

One summer day in the '80s, Stewart was happily riding his

Tuff Burner up and down Dunbar Street, while eating a salad cream sandwich (his favourite snack, bizarrely). Too focused on his salad cream sandwich and not looking where he was going, he turned down the lane and smacked into a bollard, fell off and landed on his head. The upshot was blood and salad cream everywhere.

Photos from my brother's birthday party the following day show him blowing out the candles on his cake with a giant bandage wrapped round his head. He looks like Mr Bump who, coincidentally, was his favourite *Mr Men* character.

For the most part though, Mr Bump and I led charmed lives. When we weren't out gallivanting on our bikes, we were kicking a football around the garden. Then, for two weeks each summer, our back patio became Centre Court at Wimbledon as we rallied with our plastic tennis rackets and yellow foam ball. I was Ivan Lendl, my brother was Stefan Edberg and I showed him no mercy as I hit him with another overhead smash.

He put up with a lot, my brother. My seniority was a source of pain for him. Whenever we played football, he was forced to spend the bulk of the time in goals, so that I could practise my penalty kicks. Never once did he complain. I was two and a half years older than Stewart, which meant he was there to be bossed about.

The two of us shared a bedroom for the best part of fifteen years, from the time he turned up in a cot until the day I left home and went to university. Stewart followed suit, but to another city. We got jobs and did things differently and now here we are, me pushing forty and him not far behind … a far cry from the brothers who biked up and down Dunbar Street.

We're still close, even if we do live hundreds of miles apart (me in Glasgow, him back in the Hopeman area). My brother is my best friend and I'd like to think I'm his. In fact, I'm pretty sure I am, especially since I don't make him go in goals any more. Our busy lives prevent us from seeing each other as often as we'd like to, but it's always fun when we do catch up.

Yet I sometimes wish we could return to those endless days when we rode our bikes together. Life is good now, but it was pretty much perfect then, and simple, really. At least, it seemed that way.

The only way to effect a return is through memory, but what if you could go back for a bit, do something that would take you there?

The biggest thing we shared besides our bedroom and the love of our parents was our love of bicycles, but where had that gone in the intervening years? I'd not had a bike since I was a teenager, and hadn't seen my brother in months. The thought struck me and I couldn't help myself. I called him up.

'Hey, Stewart.'

'Aye, Gary.'

'Fancy going out to play on our bikes?'

'Eh? I've not got a bike and neither do you.'

'Let's get some then!'

'Where would we go?'

'Up Dunbar Street.'

'Ha. Then what?'

'Duffus! We'll cycle to Duffus.'

'It's been a long while since I cycled to Duffus.'

Ah, he knew what cycling to Duffus meant. He'd been there that Christmas morning many moons ago, trying to win the Yellow Jersey on his brand new Racer.

Confident that I had my brother on my side – and that he had no choice – I fleshed out the details of a proposed bike trip, making it up as I went along.

We'd set off from the back gate of our old house on Dunbar

Street and pedal to Duffus, but we wouldn't stop there. No, we'd carry on to Elgin, and that wouldn't be the end of it either. We'd go right round the country and end up back where we started, at the back gate of our old house on Dunbar Street.

'That'll take a while,' said Stewart.

'Aye, but are you up for it?'

'Och, might as well.'

He's a good sport, my brother, went along with everything I said when we were kids and was now going to put up with this palaver on wheels.

Speaking of wheels, I needed to get my hands on a bike.

I popped down to my local bike shop in Glasgow to see what I could find. I explained what I was looking for, something that might carry me round the country despite my questionable fitness.

Joe the bike man suggested a hybrid bike. I nodded to show that I knew what that meant. I figured it was half bike and half something else. Horse, motorbike, biscuit …

The first bike Joe showed me had no mane, engine or choco-late topping. Besides these deficiencies, it was the greenest bike I'd ever seen.

Joe moved on to other bike models in more subtle shades, but I kept coming back to the big green monster in the corner of the room. My initial reaction had been 'no way'. Now I'd decided I was getting it.

'I'll take the green one,' I said and Joe congratulated me on my choice. Besides being green, the bike would supposedly serve me well in different road conditions. Joe said it was very zippy too.

I tried to imagine myself being very zippy, but couldn't quite get there.

Still, it had twenty-four gears, which was twenty-one more than my Grifter XL had given me. I was happy to take all the gears I could get, given the country I was planning to cover wasn't particularly known for being flat.

I took a picture of my new bike and texted it to my brother.

'The Green Lantern!' Stewart texted back.

Joe then sorted me out with a few other bike essentials. Things I hadn't quite got round to thinking about, like a helmet, a pump, a lock, a water bottle, a puncture repair kit and a neat little saddle bag.

'What about panniers?' asked Joe.

Ah, I knew what they were, but I didn't need them. I was intending to cycle round Scotland with a small backpack on my back. To be fair, Joe didn't think this ridiculous, or at least he didn't say so. I left the bike shop with his best wishes, my new bike and all the other stuff he'd picked out.

Cycling home along the canal towpath, I only had two near collisions with local youths. One said 'sorry mate' as if it were his fault and the other one called me a 'bawbag'. Which was fair enough really as I was still getting the hang of this thing.

When I got back home, my four-year-old daughter Isabella and eighteen-month-old son Alexander were playing in the back garden. I showed them Daddy's new bike and imagined future bike rides together.

Meanwhile, Stewart had gone to his nearest bike shop in Elgin to see about a set of wheels. He'd also been recommended one of these half mountain bike, half road bike hybrid numbers on which to scoot around the country.

'What colour is it?' I asked.

'White.'

'White?'

'Aye, white.'

A White Knight to my Green Lantern ... not quite a Tuff Burner and a Grifter XL but, hey, we had to be realistic. We needed to be able to go further than the top of Dunbar Street.

Now that we had the means, we required a solid plan, something like a proper route with daily destinations, an A to B and the rest of it.

I went on the internet and happened across a bike forum that featured some hair-raising posts about the experience of cycling on Scotland's roads. Some of those first-hand accounts scared the wits out of me and I developed an instant aversion to A-roads.

Thankfully I found out about the National Cycle Network, which consisted of minor roads and dedicated cycle paths. Heartened to learn of its existence, I decided we should be sticking to it as much as possible.

No doubt we'd have to contend with main roads at some point – particularly in rural areas where there might only be one road – but nevertheless, I was keen to minimise the risks. This bike trip wasn't worth doing if one or the other of us was going to get hurt – and my brother is the most accident-prone person I know.

In addition to splitting his head after crashing his bike into a bollard while eating a salad cream sandwich, he has broken a knee, a toe, more than one rib and swallowed his tongue, all playing football. He also broke his collarbone while dressed up as Batman and trying to jump over a fence in an Arran beer garden. I've got the jump on video, actually. It ends with Batman lying on the ground clutching his shoulder and the voice of his best pal Dougie in the background, going 'ooh, bad Batman'. Batman spent the rest of the night in the corner of the pub with an ice pack on his shoulder, while the rest of us got steadily drunker. No one thought to consider that Batman may have done himself a proper injury.

Well, if he was coming on this bike trip, he wasn't to bring a Batman costume or a football, and neither was he to pack any salad cream sandwiches. Really though, what was I even thinking, bringing him on this journey? Oh yes, that's right, he's my brother.

Still fretting about my injury-prone sibling, I ordered some maps from Sustrans, the sustainable transport charity behind the National Cycle Network. When the maps came, I thought it a pity they didn't highlight every bollard in Scotland. Still, they looked sturdy and I was delighted to discover that the cycle network ran through Elgin. We'd be able to join it there.

Hopeman to Aberdeen looked to be about 100 miles as the cyclist flies. The route skirted the Moray coast for a while before cutting inland through Aberdeenshire to the Granite City. We'd never manage that in one day – not the first day, anyway – but we could do it in two, surely?

From Aberdeen, we'd cycle down the east coast to Edinburgh, then pedal over to Glasgow. We would then cycle north to Inverness, which would put us within touching distance of Hopeman, but we wouldn't head home just yet. We'd push on to the top of the mainland and wind our way back from Durness via the Black Isle, to the back gate of our old house on Dunbar Street.

The entire journey clocked in at around 1,000 miles, a similar distance as from Land's End to John O'Groats – except we'd just have Scottish hills and Scottish weather to contend with.

Och, we'd be fine.

The key, surely, was to break those 1,000 miles into digestible daily chunks. I reckoned we could handle 50 or 60 miles a day, 70 at a push. Though it would be these sorts of distances, day in, day out, for a fortnight.

How many miles had I cycled in the past twenty years?

Yet it all looked so manageable on a map: roads the length of a pencil ... two-dimensional hills ...

I thought I should phone my brother and fill him in on the details, give him some sort of indication of what he was in for (over and above having to spend two weeks in my company).

'Where's Durness?' asked Stewart.

'Up the top.'

'Shetland?'

'Nah, not that far.'

'That's okay then.'

'So you're fine with this?'

'Sounds good to me.'

I had to say he sounded very relaxed, my brother. Had he been in intensive training? He'd not long bought his bike. No, it's just the way Stewart is, unfazed by anything much, even my preposterous notions. Between him being so laid-back and me with my head in the clouds, we were approaching this journey as if we were just going round the block.

I went out on the Green Lantern a few times in the weeks leading up to the big departure. I wouldn't exactly call it train-ing, more like pedalling a mile or two along the towpath and back again, sometimes stopping for a pint along the way.

When I got wind of my brother's 30-mile rides in the Moray countryside after his work it should have prompted me into ac-tion, but it didn't. I was lucky if I was squeezing in 30 miles a week.

I'd somehow convinced myself I didn't need to train like him, despite him being the sporty one. He's a smashing footballer, Stewart. The number of times I've watched from the sidelines as he shimmied past an opponent to set up a teammate or launch a rocket towards the top corner.

Of course, I've also seen him carried off the pitch a few times with a fresh injury.

Yet he'd shown far more athleticism in his life than I ever had.

Riding a bike is the most natural thing in the world, I kept telling myself. But if you've not done much of it since you were a kid and didn't really do any other kinds of exercise besides walking and playing the occasional round of golf – which is walking – then the idea that I could simply hit the road one day and cycle 1,000 miles was a fairly flawed one.

Meanwhile, a friend had sent me a link to a YouTube clip, entitled 'Shit Cyclists Say'. Having watched it, I was able to tell anyone who happened to ask how my preparations were going that 'I'm having a recovery day today'.

So I stuck with my low-key build-up. I studied the maps, booked accommodation in the towns we'd be staying in and, if it was nice out, I'd maybe pull my bike from the shed and potter along the canal for a bit. The Green Lantern hadn't so much as seen a hill yet.

I just told myself I'd ease into it. Sure, the first day would be tough and the following day might be a sore one, but after that? It would get better.

I was so ill-equipped.

There was also the question of suitable clothing. Friends who were properly into cycling kept asking me what I was going to wear. Wear? I was going to wear a T-shirt, shorts and trainers. What else was there? Of course, I'd take a jumper and a pair of trousers to wear to the pub at night, plus a cagoule in case it rained.

But somehow this was ridiculous. Apparently I needed proper cycling gear.

I was told to invest in a cycling shirt because the special fabric worked the sweat away from your body and made you more comfortable. What, more comfortable than a T-shirt?

Someone then mentioned cycling socks and I thought they were winding me up. Could I not just wear normal socks? Or sports socks? Were cycling socks sports socks? Seemingly not.

Next thing I knew I was being told about cycling shoes. What the heck were cycling shoes?

All of this bike garb chat was beginning to freak me out.

Of course, the most recommended item of all was the one I least wanted to wear.

Cycling shorts.

No way, not a good look. I'd be wearing football shorts, thank you very much – probably my old Juventus ones, they were pretty comfy. But my mates in the know assured me that, for the sake of my arse, I must wear cycling shorts. Yes, I might think they looked daft, but the strategic padding they provided was crucial if I wanted to avoid excruciating pain throughout the trip.

A mountain biking friend said that he wore cycling shorts, but beneath baggier shorts. I could live with that, I thought. I could wear that look.

Then my wife alerted me to the fact that our local supermarket had just got in a range of cycling gear. So I went down to have a look and came back with a bunch of stuff: two cycling shirts, two pairs of shorts, two pairs of socks *and* a cycling jacket, all for fifty quid. Sorted.

I phoned my brother to tell him about my purchases and he promptly rushed down to his local branch of the same supermarket to see what he could pick up.

Then it hit me.

All the gear was in one style, in the same colours. We were going to be dressed identical, just like when we were kids and mam had us in matching tank tops and trousers. She was going to love this.

Departure day was almost upon us. We had the bikes, the gear, the maps and rooms booked in B&Bs and hostels up and down the country, in places like Montrose, Newtonmore, Ullapool and Lairg. There had never been any thought of taking a tent. Beds were the least we deserved after a long day in the saddle.

A couple of days before the Big Off, I read a newspaper interview with Chris Hoy and tried to pick up some advice from the Scottish cycling legend.

'Don't look at the top of the mountain,' said Hoy. 'Just take one step at a time and you won't be overwhelmed. You don't have to worry about the bigger picture.'

I wasn't going to worry about the bigger picture.

I was also fortunate enough to grab a quick chat with the president of Scottish Cycling, no less. Alasdair Maclennan and I follow each other on Twitter. Hearing about my impending bike trip, Alasdair said I should give him a call if I wanted any advice. I did, so I did.

Alasdair's first words lodged in my brain.

'Your arse is the most important bit of the lot.'

It was just as well I'd invested in some cycling shorts. Alasdair told me to get some anti-chafing cream too and not to be shy with it. 'Smear it on,' he said.

I hadn't imagined having this kind of conversation with the president of Scottish Cycling, but was glad I was having it, because this man knew what he was talking about, whereas I was clueless. His tips hit home. Of course I had to look after my backside. It would be bearing the brunt of this long journey.

'And take lots of sunscreen,' said Alasdair.

Well, it was sunny Scotland after all.

One of my main worries was water. I drink a lot of the stuff anyway and would be wanting to down tons of it in the coming fortnight, but all I had was the one water bottle.

'Pick up water at shops,' said Alasdair. 'Don't be loading yourself down because the weight becomes a burden. As I say to folk, when the road goes up, the laws of physics apply.'

My new cycling guru had some other nuggets of advice.

'Leave at the same time each morning, irrespective of the weather. Do two thirds of your daily target before you stop – and the last bit's a doddle. You'll feel rejuvenated. Routine is the most important thing. Get into the habit, get into the rhythm.'

Rhythm was my dancer.

'What about breakfast?' I asked. With all those B&Bs we'd

be staying in, I wondered about the wisdom or otherwise of tucking into the full Scottish before hitting the road. I wanted to know if the heid bike dude thought I should be avoiding fry-ups.

'If you want a cooked breakfast, have it,' said Alasdair. 'Don't go mad about diet. That's only for the high end.'

So sausage, bacon and black pudding it was then. I'd soon ride it off.

I thanked Alasdair and he wished us well, adding that if we ran into trouble anywhere, we should give him a call because his network of cycling contacts around the country might be able to help. What a top bloke.

The time was almost upon us. My brother was waiting in Hopeman. I made the four-hour trip north from Glasgow with my family, the Green Lantern strapped to the back of the car. Isabella wanted to know why I was taking the bike.

'Daddy's going on a wee journey,' I told her.

My wife Clare and the kids were staying in Hopeman while I panted round the country with my brother.

We got to my mam's house early evening, unpacked the car and had dinner. Once the kids were in bed, I popped over to my granny's. The first thing she did was pour me a whisky. When I'd done with that, she poured me another one.

I glanced at the clock. It was 10 p.m. In ten hours' time, I was setting off to cycle round Scotland and here I was, dramming. These whiskies were Granny measures too.

Ooft.

Chapter 1

Local heroes

Day 1 – Hopeman to Banff

I stood at the back gate of our old house on Dunbar Street, where I'd left my silver Strika that fateful lunchtime thirty years ago.

Where had the time gone? Where did my bike go? The bastard.

I looked over the gate into the garden that my brother and I played in as kids and was pleased to see the hole in the hedge at the bottom of the garden was still there. That hole – just big enough for a child to scramble through – had been the tunnel at Hampden as far as Stewart and I were concerned.

We'd fit through it with our football and emerge, wearing our Scotland strips, onto the large area of grass known as Maggie's Green. Maggie was the old lady who lived in the house on the other side of the green. She and her husband George would stand at their back wall and watch my brother and me play. Stewart was in goals, of course. When we were done, Maggie would give us a sweetie.

Maggie's Green is long gone now. A house stands on our field of dreams.

I turned to my brother. He certainly looked the part in his brand new bike gear. Stewart had put on his red cycling shirt. The other one he'd bought, the white one, was in his bag. I was wearing my white cycling shirt and had the red one in reserve. We'd consulted each other before getting dressed that morning.

I did feel awkward though. It was the awkwardness of wearing cycling shorts for the first time. I had them on under baggy shorts, but they felt strange. I'd get used to them. I realised they were going to save my behind. The anti-chafing cream had been applied too. Oh, the glamour.

It was just past eight o'clock on a Sunday morning in late May. The sun was shining and we'd drawn quite a crowd of well-wishers, all here to give us a good send-off. Mam was here, our sister Julieann too, my wife and children, Granny, Great Auntie Minnie … and Auntie Ishbel!

Maybe Auntie Ishbel could hold on to the back of my bike while I readied myself to set off. Just like old times. There were no nettles on Dunbar Street, as far as I could see.

'That's some colour of bike,' said Auntie Ishbel.

She was right, it really was the most lurid green.

'Look after yourselves,' said Mam.

'You'll both have sore bums by the time you get to Elgin,' chipped in our sister. Julieann is the youngest of the three of us and had reminded Stewart and me that we never used to let her have a go on our bikes. I think she was more than happy to be missing out on this trip though.

I gave Clare a kiss, and Isabella and Alexander too. I was going to miss them. Just then, the miss was bigger than the task I'd set myself.

'Enjoy yourselves,' said Clare.

'Bye, Daddy,' said Isabella, and my heart melted.

Alexander just stared. He'd no clue what was going on, much like his dad.

I took a sip from my water bottle and stuck it back in the holder.

Then I glanced down the lane and saw the bollard that my brother had had his argument with all those years ago.

Of all the people to take on a bike ride round Scotland, even if he was the only person I was ever going to take. He kept finding new and more eye-watering ways of hurting himself.

Suddenly I remembered that time he survived a football match unscathed, only to flirt with serious injury after the final whistle. Seemingly out of harm's way, he was helping take down the nets when he jumped up and caught a ring he was wearing on one of the hooks holding up the net. Luckily it was a cheap ring and it broke and my brother didn't lose a finger. It was just staved.

And this hazard with a capital HAZARD was my preferred cycling partner. To be honest, I felt invincible next to him. Nothing was ever going to happen to me while Stewart was in tow.

We were just getting ready to set off when a van drew up. It was only Mario!

Stewart and I used to work for Mario, making ice cream. It was the coolest job ever for a kid. Mario ran the Hopeman café, where I spent most of my youth. When I wasn't making ice cream, I was lobbing coins into the arcade machines – Bubble Bobble was a favourite – or ordering a king rib supper at the chip counter. To this day, I'm not entirely sure what a king rib is.

My brother worked for Mario longer than I did. Stewart loved making ice cream. He and Mario had gone to London once for a national ice cream competition and picked up an award in the strawberry category.

'Where are you pair off to?' asked Mario, wondering about the bikes.

'Just a wee ride round the country,' I said.

'Would you mind dropping this stuff off in Lossie for me first?' Mario asked.

Stewart and I laughed. Mario was making his morning ice cream deliveries. All those times my brother and I had helped him drop off flavours to shops across Moray.

The only delivery we would be making today was the safe delivery of ourselves to a Banff B&B.

Mario wished us all the best and drove on up Dunbar Street. It was good to see him. He always reminded me of my youth, my happy ice cream days.

What about Auntie Ishbel though? She'd only gone and fashioned a starting line for us, holding up one end of her scarf while her sister – our mam – held the other end. We were departing Hopeman in style.

My brother and I got our bikes in position.

'On your marks …' shouted Auntie Ishbel. She was a good shouter. We didn't need a starting pistol.

'Get set …'

This was it. I smiled at my kids and they returned looks of bemusement.

'Go!'

That was that, then.

My brother and I pedalled up Dunbar Street together for the first time in almost thirty years. We turned round for one last look at our folks, waving to us from outside the house we grew up in. We then focused on the road ahead before either of us clattered into a parked car.

What lay ahead these next fifteen days? One thousand miles, was the short answer.

We reached the top of Dunbar Street and continued along Golf Road. I was just about to say something to Stewart when another voice said 'Aye, aye', and we'd another cyclist alongside us.

It was only Oog! Oog had grown up on Dunbar Street too. He was a couple of years older than us and Oog was only his nickname. We'd always looked up to him, partly because he was older and taller, but also because he was Oog. He used to stop and play football with us and give us praise when we scored. Oog was magic in our eyes and here he was now, right at the point at which we were trying to relive our childhoods. What an amazing coincidence. First Mario, now Oog, within minutes of each other. It felt like my entire life was flashing before me. The next thing I hoped to see was my silver Strika.

Oog was just back from the harbour. He'd been up at the crack of dawn and out on the Moray Firth, checking his creels on this glorious morning.

'Heaven on earth,' said Oog as he cycled beside us and I didn't doubt him. Then, 'See you boys', and off he went home.

'Oog,' smiled my brother as we watched him go.

A minute later, we'd left Hopeman. It's a small place, but full of characters and fond memories.

My brother and I cycled past the golf course and then took the turn-off to Duffus, just as we had that Christmas morning many years ago.

A family of cyclists was heading towards us. The children looked happy, and why wouldn't they be? We all said hello on this ideal morning for it, with zero breeze and not a cloud in the sky.

Stewart and I breezed through Duffus, hitting the two-mile mark and reaching the limit of our previous shared cycling experience. We'd never cycled further than this point together before.

We were now bound for Elgin. We'd both done Hopeman to Elgin countless times in a car and a fair few times on the bus. I used to catch the bus up to Elgin on a Saturday afternoon to spend my ice cream earnings on records from Woolies. My first girlfriend was from Elgin, too. In the summer months, I'd cycle up from Hopeman to see her. I knew every inch of this road.

There wasn't much traffic this early Sunday morning, just the occasional car or tractor. We cycled past a field where my brother and I once spent the October holidays picking tatties. Boy, was that back-breaking work. I remember being paid by the farmer at the end of the day and thinking the reward didn't match the pain. Making ice cream was much more fun.

We passed the ruins of Duffus Castle where we used to roll our eggs down the mound at Easter. I had a sudden memory of us scooping tadpoles from the moat and into a jar.

'A wasp just hit me on the mouth,' said Stewart, cycling in front of me.

'At least it didn't sting you,' I said.

It would have been just like him to kick off the bike trip with a wasp sting.

Stewart was setting a sensible pace. Perhaps it could remain this way, with me cycling in his slipstream, conserving energy. I knew how it was done. I'd seen the cycling on the telly. Pedalling behind my brother also meant he'd reach the pub first and could get the first round in.

'My bike's squeaking,' said Stewart.

It was too.

'You sure that thing's roadworthy?' I asked.

'I only just got it.'

'Maybe you should get it checked.'

'Is it okay if we pop into the bike shop in Elgin?'

'Sure. You can't be riding a squeaky bike for the next fortnight.'

We came to Kintrae Brae.

'Here we go,' said Stewart.

Kintrae Brae is a bloody big brae. It was a tough challenge as a kid and it presented one now. I put some of the Green Lantern's twenty-four gears to good use and made it to the top without having to get off. I noted how my brother had taken Kintrae Brae in his stride.

We entered Elgin, passing a hall that used to hold record fairs. I'd once picked up Prince's *Black Album* on vinyl for fifteen quid of my ice cream money. I was heavily into Prince as a teenager. When I was seventeen, I went all the way down to Manchester on the train to see him in concert for the first time, dragging my brother along with me. I can't believe we were allowed to go. I remember we stayed with nuns near the venue. I've no idea how I arranged that. What a bizarre trip that was. The places I take my little brother.

His pals teased him for attending a Prince concert, but now he's as big a fan as I am. We've seen him a few times together in Glasgow and in London, although Stewart hasn't danced on stage with Prince, like I have.

We cycled past Borough Briggs, the home of Elgin City FC. My brother and I once watched them thrash East Stirlingshire 5–1 in a Scottish Third Division match. Elgin City wear black and white stripes and I call them the Juventus of the North. Nobody else does.

Now we were passing Elgin Town Hall, of which I have many fond memories. I was a teenage thespian, a member of Moray Youth Theatre. Every year we performed a musical for three nights running before a sell-out audience.

My first role was a big one. At the age of twelve, I landed the part of Oliver and asked for more. Another time, we did *The Wizard of Oz* and I got to be the Tin Man. That role really suited me, as my dancing was rusty anyway. The Cowardly Lion was brilliant – he had to be because he was played by Kevin McKidd, an Elgin boy who would go on to become a major film and TV star. In fact, I loaned Kevin my Prince *Sign "O" The Times* video on the steps of Elgin Town Hall in 1989 and have yet to get it back!

We got to the bike shop and my brother popped in to see if they could make his bike stop squeaking. A guy had a quick look, did something to it and handed it back.

'Should be fine now,' he said.

'Cheers,' said Stewart.

Out in the car park, we got chatting to a man who'd just climbed off his bike. He asked where we were bound for. We told him about our plans to cycle round the country.

'Where are you heading?' Stewart asked him.

'Anderson & England,' said the man, pointing to the furniture store across the road.

My brother and I got back on our bikes – the White Knight now squeakless, thank goodness – and pedalled through Cooper Park, passing the pond with its ducks and pedalos. It had been a long time since I'd been in a pedalo, but we didn't have the time.

We passed the ruins of Elgin Cathedral, once the second largest cathedral in the country. It was torched in the fourteenth century by the Wolf of Badenoch, who wasn't a real wolf but a man called Alexander Stewart, the Earl of Buchan, who had a beef with the Bishop of Moray.

We were just about leaving Elgin now and I'd time for one last memory, and not a pleasant one at that. We were near the site of the Bishops, an Elgin nightspot popular in its day. My worst night out ever started and ended there, a night that was over before it got going.

I was eighteen and on my first pint of the evening when I went to the toilet and collapsed in a cubicle. My world spinning wildly, I vaguely remember then crawling around the car park.

My pals were inside having the time of their lives and had no idea where I was. I barely knew where I was. Someone had spiked my drink.

I somehow got home in a taxi and ended up being bedded for three days and missing most of my university Freshers' Week. Good times, eh?

Now we were out of Elgin and cycling along a back road towards the village of Garmouth. The Green Lantern was riding fine. The bag on my back felt comfortable too. Its contents were: a spare cycling shirt, spare cycling shorts, spare cycling socks, my cycling jacket, a cagoule, a jumper, a pair of trousers, a few rolled-up T-shirts, some pants and regular socks, toiletries, sunscreen, anti-chafing cream, midge spray, route maps, notebook and pen, phone charger. I think that was it.

My tiny saddle bag contained my wallet, phone, a puncture repair kit, house keys (we were spending the night in Glasgow at my place) and key for the D-lock which was mounted on my bike frame next to my water bottle.

Stewart was travelling similarly lightly and had also brought some travel wash which might come in handy. When we reached Glasgow in six days' time, we would replenish our bags with fresh clothes, maybe doing a proper wash overnight. We'd gone as far as sharing toiletries in an attempt to be as streamlined as possible – one tube of toothpaste, one small bottle of shampoo. Neither of us had brought shaving foam or razor blades. We were just going to become beardy.

By the time we got to Garmouth, we had a terrible thirst. The day was young, but it was already hot. Our bottles were empty and we were struggling to find a shop. When we did find one, it was shut, permanently. This was no good.

We stopped a man walking past and asked him. He pointed us towards a shop we'd somehow missed. He was going there now to pick up his paper. He asked where we'd come from and we told him Hopeman.

'I love it up here,' he said, telling us he was originally from a rough part of Glasgow. 'It's okay,' he added. 'I won't batter you.' This nice man, who wasn't going to batter us, collected his paper and we got our hands on some water.

'Be safe and enjoy yourselves,' said the man. 'If the weather's like this, you should have a great time.'

We said cheerio to him and slapped on some sunscreen. It was turning out to be a scorcher, one of the finest days of the year so far. We might just have timed it right with our late May departure. Mind you, we had another fourteen days ahead of us. They'd all be filled with rain, wouldn't they?

Just after Garmouth, we crossed the River Spey on an amazing old railway bridge that sparkled in the sun.

'*Stand By Me*,' said Stewart, and I knew exactly what he meant. There is a key scene in that coming-of-age '80s movie where the kids walk across a viaduct not unlike this one.

Instead of carrying on after the bridge, we took a wee detour down to Spey Bay, where the river enters the Moray Firth. The Scottish Dolphin Centre is at Spey Bay. I'd been wanting to visit for some time, but had never quite got round to it. Since we were here, it was the perfect opportunity. Maybe I'd see a dolphin for the first time too. Despite growing up on the Moray coast, I'd never seen the celebrated dolphins of the Moray Firth. It was a ridiculous state of affairs and something I couldn't quite work out.

'Never seen them either,' shrugged Stewart, which was doubly ridiculous.

Had we spent our whole childhoods with our backs to the sea? The firth was full of dolphins. Maybe it was simply bad luck. If we could just see a dolphin on the first day of our bike trip, that would be something.

Before we got to the dolphin centre, we passed a golf course.

'Dad and I played there once,' said Stewart.

'You did?'

'Aye, after our round we got steadily pissed in the bar and hustled at pool.'

'Sounds like a cracking day out.'

'Aye, it was.'

Dad loved his golf. He liked a pint too. It was hard to believe it was five years since he'd passed away.

As we reached the dolphin centre, a siren went off.

'Dolphins!' I thought. Must be some kind of dolphin alert system to indicate they'd shown up in the bay. Then I realised it was someone's car alarm.

We parked our bikes by a dyke and, following the disappoint-
ment of the false car alarm, I made my first dolphin spot: an
inflatable one lying on the grass.

The non-inflatable dolphins of the Moray Firth are the only
resident population of bottlenose dolphins in the North Sea,
and the most northerly dolphins in the world. There are more
than a hundred of the flipping things and we'd yet to see one
of them.

'I saw a seal once,' said Stewart.

'That doesn't count.'

The dolphins like to swing by Spey Bay to feast on salmon at
the mouth of the river. It was a good spot for a dolphin centre.

A sign read: 'If you do see dolphins please let us know.' If I saw
a dolphin, I was fairly going to shout about it.

I wandered across to a mounted telescope pointed out to the
sea. I peered through it, hoping to see a dolphin waving back
at me, but no, although I could see Lossiemouth, where my
brother and I went to school.

The volunteer researchers at the dolphin centre spend their
days collecting information on the dolphins. How often they
visit, how many there are, what sort of music they're currently
into. Stewart and I got chatting to Charlotte, one of the volunteers. We told her we were from Hopeman and that we'd never
seen a dolphin.

'There are people who live just up the road here at Spey Bay
who've never seen dolphins,' smiled Charlotte.

That made us feel better, knowing that there were other people local to the area who were just as rubbish at spotting dolphins as we were.

'You're either looking or it's completely by chance you see
them,' said Charlotte. 'But this is a great place to spot them.
There are loads of salmon at the river mouth and the dolphins
come here and have an absolute feast.'

'Seen many dolphins lately?' I asked.

'We've had them five days in a row so far,' said Charlotte. 'They were here this morning. They disappeared off, but they might come back. Fingers crossed!'

Up here for the summer, Charlotte was from Canterbury in Kent.

'Not many dolphins there,' said Stewart.

'No,' she laughed.

With no dolphins kicking about, Charlotte showed us a table of marine specimens which included the skull of a dolphin and the tooth of a sperm whale. I was invited to pick up the tooth of the sperm whale.

'It's heavy,' I said.

'They have forty of these,' said Charlotte.

'You'd think it would weigh them down.' I was some way off becoming a marine biologist.

We left Charlotte to get on with her work and had a look round the rest of the dolphin centre. I went inside to sign the guestbook, but my brother stopped me.

'That's not the guestbook,' said Stewart.

I looked more closely at the entries. If it was the guestbook, two dolphins had dropped by at half past nine, along with a couple of harbour porpoises. None of them had been moved to comment because it was a logbook of marine sightings.

It was time we got moving. So far we'd seen zero dolphins and cycled 15 miles, which wasn't a great deal – and we'd nearly run out of morning.

According to the route map, it was another 30 miles to Banff. I'd wanted to make this first day easy enough, but there was easy enough and taking things too easy. We were behaving like we were on holiday. We'd also promised Stewart's girlfriend Elaine that we'd stop by Portessie. Her mam was making us lunch. At this rate, it was going to be a very late lunch.

A couple of quick miles later and we were in Portgordon, one of the many fishing villages that line the Moray coast. Stewart and I come from a long line of fishermen. Dad was the skipper of a fishing boat, and Granda before him, though neither of us had followed suit.

My brother requested a stop by the sea wall on Stewart Street so he could have his picture taken next to the street sign: Stewart on Stewart Street, squinting in the sun against a backdrop of turquoise water and bright blue sky.

'Bonnie day,' said Stewart.

Over the road was a pub, a typical Scottish boozer where you couldn't see in the windows. The door was open though and I could just make out a punter standing at the bar in a Scotland top. I was 99 per cent sure he was drinking Tennent's Lager.

We weaved our way through Portgordon and pressed on along the coast. Before long, we were met by the 'Welcome to Buckie' sign. We cycled past rows of houses, gable end to the sea, a common sight in the sea towns of the Moray coast.

The smell of fish in Buckie – the biggest fishing port for miles around – was strong. We passed a seafood supplier whose blackboard had the day's specials: rock turbot, scallops and monkfish.

Being sons of a fisherman, my brother and I were raised on catches from the North Sea. Plates of lemon sole would be put on the kitchen table and we'd think 'not fish again', not realising how lucky we were. When it wasn't lemon sole, it was cod or haddock and sometimes Dad would make a pan of fish soup, one of the most memorable smells of my childhood.

Down by Buckie's harbour, we passed a ship's chandler. There used to be one of those at Hopeman harbour. A boat sat on the slip at the shipyard in Buckie and it jogged a memory of Dad's boat, the *Adonis*, undergoing some work here.

The *Adonis* normally sailed out of Peterhead. The way I remembered it, Dad had sailed the boat from Peterhead to Buckie for it to be worked on and I'd joined him and his crew. It's not as if the boat was far out in the North Sea, but I was still sick all the way, confined to a cramped berth for most of the voyage, lying under an old blanket with a bucket beside me, the smell of vomit mixing with the whiff of diesel. God, what an awful trip that was. I never sailed again and my dad never encouraged me to.

Dad's boat was Buckie-registered. BCK 85 was the number on the *Adonis* until Dad adopted INS 75, which had been the number on Granda's boat, the *Onward*. Details you never forget.

At school, I used to draw pictures of Dad's boat on the back of my jotters. Stewart did the same, though his sketches were slightly better than mine, since he was the superior artist. We may not have gone to sea, but we were most certainly proud sons of a skipper.

We were around two hours later than we said we'd be, arriving at Elaine's parents' house in Portessie. Elaine and her mam Evelyn were looking out for us, sitting on a rock overlooking the sea, enjoying the mid-afternoon sunshine. What a spot, I thought.

'How are the two of you getting on?' smiled Elaine.

'Okay,' sighed Stewart.

He spoke for both of us. We hadn't cycled far, only the smallest portion of the whole, but it was the first day and this heat was really getting to us. It was roasting.

'You'll be hungry, the pair of you,' said Evelyn. 'Come on in for a bacon roll.'

A bacon roll … I almost keeled over just thinking about it.

My brother and I staggered across the road and into the house, behind Elaine and her mam.

That was the other thing, we'd not eaten since a bacon roll at mam's first thing in the morning. We had to take better care of ourselves. Maybe we could get by on bacon rolls for fifteen days?

The smell of the frying bacon was so good it nearly knocked me out. Elaine poured us large tumblers of orange juice and we gulped it down. We were given our bacon rolls and I noticed how the rolls were a funny shape, different from rolls I'd seen before.

'Belly-button rolls,' explained Elaine. 'From the local baker's.'

'Alex Ferguson likes them,' said her mam. 'He gets them sent down to Manchester.'

I chewed on my roll. If they were good enough for Fergie ...

Afterwards, Stewart and I went and sat down in the cool, dark living room where the golf was on the telly. This was a mistake because neither of us wanted to get up. Still, we accepted re-filled tumblers of orange juice, as well as packets of Quavers and some Tunnock's Caramel Wafers.

'This is the life,' said Stewart.

'Aye,' I replied.

I wasn't taking in any of the golf on the telly. My head was scrambled with all that heat and cycling. Stewart groaned.

We really didn't wish to go anywhere, but the fact was we had to. It was another 20 miles to blooming Banff and it had now gone four o'clock.

How time flies when you're not exactly flying.

'We'd better go,' I said, quite possibly for the third time.

'Aye, we'd better,' said Stewart, opening another packet of Quavers.

Eventually we managed to separate ourselves from the couch and remove ourselves from the cool, dark living room.

On the way out of the house, I clocked the calendar on the kitchen wall.

'No way,' I said.

It was a picture of Cathedral Cove in New Zealand. I couldn't have mistaken it for anywhere else. Years ago – way before chil-dren – my wife and I had gone on a round-the-world trip and spent a fun few weeks in New Zealand. One day, staying on the Coromandel Peninsula, we'd got up and fancied going for a cycle. We hired bikes and cycled to one of the most spellbinding beaches we had ever set eyes on. We didn't know the name of the beach, but we'd then made the short walk to Cathedral Cove which turned out to be every bit as stunning as it looked now on this calendar in Elaine's mam's kitchen.

How surreal to be standing here in my cycling gear with this surprise photo reminder of one of the standout days of our round-the-world trip, a day that had been made by our decision to hire wheels. Bicycles really do make the world go round.

Having finished telling Elaine about Cathedral Cove, I apologised to her for taking her boyfriend away for the next fifteen days. I promised to look after him and bring him back to Hopeman in one piece, even though she knew fine well how injury-prone he was.

'They're all football injuries,' shrugged Stewart. 'I've never been hurt on a bicycle.'

'What about the bollard?' I reminded him.

'Oh aye.'

After throwing on more sunscreen and saying cheerio to Elaine and her mam, we climbed back on the bikes. Just past Portessie, we happened upon a busy beach scene. Folk really were making the most of this fine weather. There were people throwing beach balls back and forth, people playing cricket. This wasn't Scotland. Where in the blazes were we?

As we continued along the coastline it became ever more spectacular. Huge slanted rocks jutted out of the sea, some of them looking like they'd been sliced by a giant knife. They were the most weird and wonderful shapes. One looked like the jaws of a crocodile. I was gobsmacked.

The views grew ever more ridiculous as we found ourselves on a cliff-top path looking back to the village of Findochty.

There was so much to take in. Away in the distance were tiny houses fronted by a beach of golden sand. Right in front of us were yellow gorse bushes, reminding us of Hopeman. And down below, between the bushes and the far-off beach, was the bluest sea, rising from it immense stacks of rock.

'It's like the Twelve Apostles,' remarked Stewart.

He wasn't far off. This was the Moray coast, but it wasn't a million miles from that celebrated stretch of Australian coastline. This was something else. I couldn't believe I'd never clapped eyes on it before. We weren't that far from Hopeman. It had just taken this bike trip to get us here. This mindblowing sight made me excited about the next fourteen days. What all were we going to see?

We'd both been to the Twelve Apostles and felt qualified to make a favourable comparison. My time in Australia, on my round-the-world trip, had passed without incident. The same couldn't be said for my brother on his year Down Under. It wasn't any of Australia's dangerous creatures that got to him, he was his own worst enemy.

First there was the head injury. He'd been out drinking in Cairns with his best friend Dougie who, come to think of it, always seemed to be around when Stewart got hurt. I was quite glad I hadn't invited Dougie on this bike trip.

Anyway, the pair of them returned to their hostel to find a pool party in full swing. In an attempt to sober up, Dougie did a somersault into the water. Not to be outdone, my brother followed suit. He was mid-air when he got the call from Dougie: 'No Stewart, that's the shallow end!'

My brother hit the bottom of the pool and lost some blood. There was no salad cream involved. He woke up the next morning with toilet roll stuck to his head and the news that a cyclone was heading their way. My brother and his pals fled south in their hired car.

Once things had calmed down, they joined a three-day cruise of the Whitsunday Islands, but that didn't go too well either. On the first morning, my brother rose early and thought it might be a nice idea to sit out on deck with a cup of coffee and watch the sun rise. He had just sat down when the boat took a pitch. Stewart was flung across the deck and narrowly avoided going overboard by ramming his foot on the railing. Though that wasn't what broke his foot.

While his foot was striking the railing, his coffee cup was flying through the air. True to form, it smashed into his foot. Cup broken, foot broken. My brother spent the rest of the cruise stuck on the boat, while everyone else got to check out the Great Barrier Reef.

'Did I tell you about the time I broke my big toe playing football?' asked Stewart as we pushed on to Portknockie.

'Hmm, not sure.' It really was hard to keep track of my brother's injuries.

'Some animal stamped on it. You can't do anything with a broken toe. It's still wonky.'

'How's the pedalling going?'

'Okay, I think.'

Honest to goodness.

'Did you not once break your metatarsal or something playing football?' I asked.

'Aye, that was my fault,' confirmed Stewart. 'I kicked someone else.'

Gazing down on Portknockie, we saw kids splashing about in the harbour and having fun. It reminded me of us mucking about at Hopeman harbour when we were wee. There were various points along the pier you could jump off and they all had names like the Point, the Bunion, the Big Steps and the Eelies' Cave. Some jumps I could never work up the courage for and the water was always freezing too. There was one jump off

the back of the harbour wall that was total madness. It requ
pinpoint accuracy to hit the water between two slightly sub-
merged rocks. This jump was called the Coffin.

Then you had the 'bombing' of the Go-Gos. The Go-Gos
were the pupils of nearby Gordonstoun public school, where
various royals – including Prince Charles – were educated. The
school kept a couple of sailing boats in Hopeman harbour so
that the Go-Gos could take to the Moray Firth and learn sea-
manship.

Whenever they were leaving the harbour or returning, some
Hopeman daredevil would jump in the water as near as possible
to the vessel with the intention of soaking these posh-kid sailors.
This was the bombing of the Go-Gos. There was more chance
of the dive bomber getting hurt than the Go-Gos ever getting
wet, plus they'd been out at sea anyway. They must have thought
we were a right bunch of savages.

After more rugged cliffs and pretty coves, we reached the
town of Portsoy and wound our way down to the harbour,
where we were met with a lively scene. The tables outside the
Shore Inn were packed with folk musicians playing a host of instruments, with a crowd enjoying the tunes and sunshine while
having a drink.

'Far's yer banjo, min?' an old man asked me as I stepped off
my bike.

I laughed. There's no way I could have carried a banjo all this
way, never mind been able to play one. My brother and I decided to reward ourselves with a drink. A half pint each would
do us. Any more and we'd be in trouble.

I ordered the drinks at the bar while Stewart went off to the
toilet. When he came back, a man at the bar turned round to
him and said: 'Christ, you've changed!'

My brother didn't know quite what to say. He'd never met
this man in his life. Neither had he just had a change of clothing.

It was a surreal moment, though, by the look of it, Stewart's new friend was several sheets to the wind.

We took our drinks outside and savoured them with the live music and harbour setting. Then we returned to the Green Lantern and White Knight before they thought we were neglecting them.

The two of us were liking our new bikes, which was probably a good thing. I wouldn't have said they were making the journey effortless. A fair degree of effort had been involved so far, what with the heat and the odd hill. But at least it wasn't windy. I was glad not to have to contend with that difficulty on the first day.

Our next town was Cullen, a place we were both familiar with. Cycling along the grand viaduct on our approach to the town, we gazed down on the golf course which my brother and I had once played as we joined forces as part of Team Hopeman.

It was a match between Hopeman juniors and Cullen juniors. We'd won the home leg convincingly, thrashing our Cullen counterparts 7–1 (it was teams of eight). We then travelled down the coast for the return leg and were hammered 8–0, therefore conceding the match.

But that wasn't the whole story. There was an awful backdrop to that game in Cullen. Since we'd defeated them in Hopeman, two of my best pals, Mark and Craig, had lost their lives in a car crash. Mark, a fine golfer, had played the match in Hopeman. I remember him standing on the first tee, in the prime of his young life.

The tragedy hit our tiny community hard. I was old enough to understand and young enough not to fully grasp it.

I remembered trying to talk to my opponent that day in Cullen, in my own inarticulate teenage way, about Mark and Craig. The boy from Cullen was as young as I was. He didn't know what to say. He beat me by the odd hole, but the outcome didn't seem to matter much.

Seeing the course now after more than twenty years, I thought about my friends, as I often do. I've now spent more of my life without them than I did with them.

I set my sadness aside and cycled into Cullen with my brother.

'Strugglin' the day?' asked a man in the street who looked like Elvis and possibly was Elvis. His quiff was a beauty. His attitude was all Elvis too. He had it all going on, except he was in Cullen.

I'd thought about treating myself to some Cullen skink while we were there, but it was much too hot for a steaming bowl of fish soup. Ice cream was a much better idea.

Everyone else, it seemed, was thinking along the same lines. We joined the queue outside the ice cream shop and, when we reached the head of it, ordered single nougat wafers. We former ice cream makers both gave the ice cream the thumbs-up. It was good and fresh. We wolfed down our nougat wafers before the ice cream melted in the sun. Then we slapped some more sunscreen on our faces, necks, arms and legs.

Back on the road and past Cullen, a tiny but incredibly noisy souped-up car with tinted windows raced past. Five minutes later, it flew by in the other direction.

But, for the most part, it was peaceful as we were treated to more epic views of a coastline you could never tire of. At one point I stopped at an information board to read about the cute local wildlife.

'Watch out for the Great Black-backed Gull,' I read. 'Head and shoulders taller than any of our other gulls, with a huge bill and a deep, harsh call …'

'Here, Stewart!' I called. 'Come and listen to this!'

'The Great Black-back is a truly fearsome bird,' I read on to my brother, 'capable of swallowing its food whole, up to the size of rabbits.'

'Bloody hell,' said Stewart.

Seemingly this winged beast killed its prey by bludgeoning it with its massive bill before ripping it apart. I read on:

'It is estimated that there are around 25,000 breeding pairs nesting around the rocky coast, on the cliff-tops or stacks.'

'Shit,' I said. 'There's loads of them.'

I looked around for any sign of the Great Black-backed Gull, checking rocks and scanning the skies too. I imagined a battalion of the feathered buggers dive-bombing us. Maybe the heat was making me delirious and causing these fevered thoughts.

Growing up on the Moray coast, I was well accustomed to the sight of seagulls. Some of them were bigger than any bird had any right to be. You always had to be extra careful scoffing a fish supper – or even a king rib supper – out in the open when there were gulls about.

But this looked like something different altogether, this mutant gull.

'It's only a bird, Gary,' said my brother.

'That's easy for you to say,' I said. 'Do you know my pal Alasdair was once attacked by a curlew when he was out cycling?'

'What's a curlew?'

'A big bird with a big beak.'

'What did your pal do?'

'He hadn't done anything.'

'No, what did he do when this bird attacked him?'

'He did all he could do. He hid behind a rock. It left him alone eventually, but Alasdair was pretty shaken up by the whole thing.'

'Does he still go out cycling?'

'Aye, but he's extra vigilant and scans the skies in case the curlew comes back for him.'

'Should we get going?'

'Aye, it's probably for the best.'

It wasn't far now to Banff, where the Great Black-backed Gulls would have less chance of picking us off.

As we cycled the final stretch, I felt my legs starting to go. The first day's efforts were beginning to catch up on me and no wonder, really. I'd done more than 40 miles in blistering heat – by Scottish standards – and some of those coastal stretches had been fairly hilly. I was pretty sure I was going to feel it come the morning. My brother seemed to have breezed through the day. He was definitely way ahead of me in terms of fitness and we knew why that was. He'd put the work in beforehand. Right now Stewart was coasting it, while I was hanging in there.

'Don't worry,' said my brother. 'You'll be fine by the fourth day.'

'I look forward to it.'

He then proceeded to tell me some tale about a man who had been hospitalised and put on a drip for two weeks after his legs nearly exploded or something.

'Weird, eh?'

'Thanks, Stewart.'

Having been freaked out by the very existence of the Great Black-backed Gull, I was now worried my legs were going to explode.

We arrived in Banff with my legs intact, passing a row of cute fishing cottages and being treated to a welcoming view of a wide sweep of sand turned golden by the low evening sun, which also lit up the neighbouring town of Macduff on the other side of the bay.

It was just past seven o'clock. We'd set off at the back of eight, which meant it had taken us eleven hours to cycle 40 or so miles. That was snail pace. Mind you, we had stopped in Elgin to get Stewart's bike looked at and had spent the best part of an hour at the dolphin centre. Another hour in Portessie feeding our faces and kicking back in a cool, dark room. A half-pint in

Portsoy and an ice cream in Cullen … perhaps the slowness was more to do with the pauses than the pace we'd kept. The point was that we were here in one piece. We'd seen through the first day.

Though we had reached our day one destination, we still had one heck of a hill to climb to reach our B&B. It was so steep, I had to get off and push. Of course, my brother remained on his bike, working his gears and demonstrating his superior strength.

Once we got to our room, the first thing Stewart did was some stretching exercises, mainly, he said, for his hamstrings. I mainly wanted a lie down, but he insisted I join him, saying that it was for my own good. It was like a mini-exercise class. Not that I'd ever been near an exercise class.

'You'll feel better in the morning,' said Stewart.

I wondered what tomorrow would bring. I feared waking up and not being able to move. Maybe this would help me out.

When I was done stretching, I wandered over to the bathroom sink and splashed cold water on my face. Immediately my eyes started to sting. I'd just washed sunscreen into them. Ouch. I squinted into the mirror. My eyes had gone cartoon bloodshot. Look at the state of me. I might not get served in the pub looking like this. They'd think I was wasted.

After showers and a change of clothes, we ventured out into the Banff night. My eyes were still nipping, but we were successfully served in the first pub we stumbled across. Food-wise, I went for the scampi basket, my brother opting for the haggis, neeps and tatties.

The Happy Mondays were playing in the background and this made me happy. The pint was making me happy too. Though, I had to say, I'd found it hard sitting down and wondered if I was ever going to be able to get back up. When we were done with our meals, the barman collected our plates in a beer crate. I'd never seen that done before.

Before heading for our beds, we walked down by the harbour for a nightcap in the Ship Inn. As we approached, we could hear loud music. Rhinestone Cowboy, for sure. It seemed there was a live band on, then I realised it was karaoke. Luckily the karaoke was in the lounge and we were able to sit in the main bar with our pints and packets of salt and vinegar crisps.

The Ship Inn had a real salty seadog feel to it. We liked it. The other thing about the Ship Inn is that it was the pub in *Local Hero*. Interior shots for the classic Scottish movie were filmed here. The place didn't look like it had changed that much.

'I've never seen *Local Hero*,' said my brother.

'You've never seen *Local Hero*?'

'Nope.'

'How can that be?'

'Well, you've never seen *E. T.*'

It's true, and I've no explanation why.

'I've not seen *Watership Down* either,' I said, taking a sip of my pint.

'I've never seen *Bambi*,' said Stewart.

We sat thinking up films we'd never seen.

'*Rambo*?'

'Aye.'

'*Sound of Music*?'

'No.'

We were now being treated to a wild rendition of 'Pour Some Sugar on Me' from the karaoke next door.

I looked over to the pool table. Hanging from the ceiling above it was a creel with Winnie the Pooh inside. Hanging next to a trapped Winnie the Pooh was Bagpuss on a surfboard, riding the crest of an imaginary wave. I couldn't recall that particular scene from *Local Hero*. At least there wasn't a Great Black-backed Gull on a bike up there too. That would have scared the bejesus out of me.

Leaving the Ship Inn, I stopped to look at a framed photograph on the wall. It was of Bill Forsyth, the director of *Local Hero*, standing behind the bar.

Walking back up the road to our B&B, I now had Dire Straits in my head instead of Def Leppard.

'Hey,' said Stewart as we climbed into our beds for what would hopefully be a decent night's sleep. 'We're sharing a bedroom again!'

Just like old times.

'Now, no sleepwalking,' I warned him.

'I'll try not to.'

My brother had done a fair amount of sleepwalking as a kid. Our Stewart used to scare the crap out of me with his night-time wanderings.

'You've grown out of it, haven't you?' I asked.

'Think so.'

'Night, night Stewart.'

'Night, night Gary.'

Perhaps I'd be woken up in the middle of the night by a show of sleepcycling.

At least the bikes were locked up safe.

Chapter 2

Scorching heat and blasted scones

Day 2 – Banff to Aberdeen

You'd think I'd have slept like a baby after my first full day's cycling since ever. But I barely slept at all, suffering a restless first night on the road. It was as if my body kept waking me up to tell me how angry it was with me. I must have managed two hours tops – hardly the ideal preparation for a 60-mile cycle to Aberdeen.

Stewart sat dressed on the edge of his bed, looking at the route map.

'Hills, hills, hills ...' he mumbled.

'Okay Stewart, I get the picture.'

He'd slept like a baby and hadn't sleepwalked or sleepcycled either, as far as we knew. He was considering putting on a second pair of cycling shorts to give his backside further protection, but in the end popped the second pair in his bag.

We stood facing each other. Both of us had put on fresh cycling tops, me going from white to red and him switching from red to white. If we kept doing this, it would all work out.

The pair of us put on some sunscreen as the forecast said it was going to be another hot one. Scotland was taking the piss. I supposed it was better than heavy rain and strong winds. We'd surely get some of that chucked at us before long.

I double-checked that I had everything.

'Wallet ... phone ...'

'Water?' grinned Stewart, who couldn't believe how much I'd drunk yesterday.

Before I returned the map to my bag, I had a quick look at it. Yep, there were hills, more than I'd anticipated. It was both a good and a bad thing that the route maps gave an indication of the kind of terrain you'd be tackling. For some reason, I had expected Aberdeenshire to be flat. It wasn't.

Worse still, I'd got the distance wrong. We had 10 more miles to cycle than I'd thought. I couldn't figure out how that had happened.

'I don't know how that's happened,' I said.

Stewart sighed and shook his head.

We went down for breakfast and had the works: sausage, bacon, black pudding and the rest. After that lot I wanted a lie-down, but it was gone nine already, and our initial aim had been to set off at the back of eight.

I remembered Alasdair – president of Scottish Cycling Alasdair and not curlew victim Alasdair – saying it was best to eat breakfast two hours before hitting the road. So we'd messed up on that front. We'd be digesting our breakfasts for the remainder of the morning in the saddle.

We settled the bill, slung our bags on our backs and set off again.

We were enveloped in a morning haar as we crossed the bridge and arrived in Macduff with sore arses. I'd expected some degree of tenderness in predictable places, and so it was. How bad would it have been though had I gone ahead and just worn my football shorts?

My legs didn't feel too stiff – thanks to my wise brother and his stretching exercises – and my shoulders also seemed okay, given that I was wearing a backpack, albeit a fairly light one.

We left the coast to cut inland and were confronted with our first hill climb of the day. It was a shock to the system, but we survived. My breakfast felt like a very recent thing, which it was.

Our first target was the town of Turriff, which was 12 miles away. We buckled down without a word. As soon as we left the coast, the haar lifted. We were clearly in for another day of bright sunshine. I wasn't sure how I felt about cycling in the heat again, but I was going to find out.

After too many hills and too few descents, we hit Turriff where we bumped into a cow, or rather the statue of a cow, in the town square. This was the Turra Coo, who was famous in these parts.

A century ago, a local farmer by the name of Robert Paterson refused to pay Lloyd George's National Insurance stamp then declined to pay the arrears of a fine imposed on him. As a result, one of Paterson's cows was poinded for public auction. A crowd gathered in Turriff's town square to witness the auction and a riot ensued. The cow escaped and Paterson was charged with breach of the peace.

The captured cow was sold in Aberdeen, then bought back by Turriff farmers who returned it to Mr Paterson. On her return to Turriff, the cow headed a triumphant procession of around 4,000 people. Daubed on the cow's back were the words 'Free! Divn't ye wish that ye were me'.

Which is how they talk in these parts. I do love a bit of Doric.

I got Stewart to take my picture with the Turra Coo then we went off in search of the nearest supermarket where we loaded up on bananas, Mars bars and water.

I stood outside the supermarket in the shade, gulping from a two-litre bottle of water.

'Waterboy,' laughed my brother.

'What?' I said, spilling some of the water down my shirt.

Stewart shook his head. 'I've never seen anyone drink so much water.'

'I'm thirsty!'

'You're going to turn into a fish.'

My brother took a couple of swigs himself and we decanted

the rest to our water bottles. To my mind, these water bottles weren't big enough. I should have added a second one to my bike.

'You should be towing one of those big water dispensers you get in offices,' said Stewart.

'Very funny.'

It wasn't funny in the slightest when we took the wrong road out of Turriff, only realising our mistake about a mile later. Forced to do some backtracking, I cursed the fact it had somehow gone midday and we were still on the edge of Turriff. It was something like 50 miles to Aberdeen! This did not bode well for the afternoon. The Granite City felt a long way off. It *was* a long way off, and the day was only going to heat up.

Making things more difficult was me complicating matters by insisting that we drop by Delgatie Castle. Stewart wanted me to forget about the castle.

'What's at the castle?' he asked. 'Dolphins?'

'No, scones.'

'I don't want a scone.'

'Well, we're having one.'

This castle was a complete mystery. Judging by the map we'd just passed it, but there had been no turn-off, no path, just trees everywhere.

'It should be right around here,' I said. 'You'd think there'd be a sign.'

Stewart was keeping quiet.

We carried on cycling – we were heading towards Turriff again – and then we saw a woman hanging out her washing in the garden of the only house for miles around.

'Let's ask her!' I cried to Stewart who had surely just about had enough of me.

I do this kind of thing all the time. I get an idea in my head and that's it.

So I asked the woman hanging out her washing where the castle was.

'Delgatie Castle?' said the woman while her dog barked like mad by her feet. She had to shout us the directions since her dog wouldn't stop barking.

'He barks when you mention the castle,' yelled the woman. 'He loves going for walks there.' She'd said 'castle' at least six times and I'd weighed in with a couple of mentions too.

She pointed us back up the hill we'd just come down, telling us exactly how to find the castle and saying 'castle' seven more times.

Her dog was going mental.

I was thinking maybe we should take the dog to the castle, but had my doubts Stewart would go along with that. Of course, we'd then have to bring the dog back.

I shouted my thanks to the woman and we pedalled on back up the hill. We entered the woods and followed a track we hadn't noticed first time round. Keeping an eye out for the fish pond and then cycling alongside it, we soon reached a big old building that looked very much like a castle.

Nodding to the gardeners, we dragged our bikes up a hundred or so steps and parked them next to a cannon in the castle courtyard.

'What are we here for again?' asked Stewart.

'Scones.'

'I could just go a scone,' said my brother.

I ignored his sarcasm.

We entered the castle and plonked ourselves down in the tea room. In an effort to raise the level of excitement, I told my brother about the castle's fine reputation for home baking.

'I read on the internet that this is one of the best places in Britain for afternoon tea.'

'Really,' said Stewart.

'Yes, I think it ranked eighteenth.'

'But I want a coffee, not tea.'

'Well, have a coffee then. I'm having one too, but we're having scones, right?'

Stewart shrugged. I pictured a tray arriving and my brother flinging his scone in my face. But he wouldn't do that. He's a nice brother, very mild-mannered and not – as far as I was aware – prone to episodes of scone rage.

I ordered our coffees and scones and the waitress brought everything over on a tray.

'What's that?' asked Stewart, pointing to a jar of clotted cream.

'It's not salad cream, if that's what you're thinking.'

We clarted our scones with cream and jam and scoffed them double quick without so much as uttering a word, until Stewart said: 'That was good.'

'See. You liked that, didn't you?'

Big fan of scones now, my brother. It's not even as if I was a big fan of scones myself. It's just that I'd read about them and decided we were having them. Now we'd had them I was happy, but the day was running away from us. We still had more miles to cycle on this hot afternoon than we had the whole of the day before. I tried not to think about it.

On the way out, we bumped into the keeper of the castle, or at least a lady who looked like she was in charge. I told her how much we had enjoyed the scones.

'Well,' she said. 'Those scones will fortify you for the brae.'

She'd just used the B word. I quizzed her about this brae. Turned out it was a big one.

'Motorbikes go down it like it's Le Mans,' she said, adding that it was an accident blackspot.

We'd be taking great care on this brae.

As we exited the castle, I clocked the turnpike staircase.

'Look,' I said to Stewart. 'A turnpike staircase.'

My brother just looked at me. He was all castled out.

Soon enough we were tackling the brae. It was a big one that seemed to rise forever. Halfway up, I saw the sad sight of flowers pinned to a tree. A minute later, an ambulance came tearing down the brae, lights flashing. It could have been for any number of reasons, but it gave me pause for thought. I wanted this brae over with and for us to be on the next part of our journey.

We got to the top and I put it down to the scone factor. I easily could have got off and pushed at some points, but I hadn't.

On the drop that followed, my brother appeared to be trying to see how many flies he could swallow, because he caught at least two of them.

'Bleurgh,' he said, or something to that effect. We were approaching the hottest part of the day. 'I'll surely be sleepwalking tonight,' said Stewart.

He went sleepwalking once on a family holiday in Spain after catching too much sun on a trip to a waterpark. He'd gone to bed, but was then found in the hotel corridor, clinging to the wall in his pyjamas and havering about the amount of cars that kept whizzing past.

My brother is the feverish type and this sun was really beginning to beat down on us now. The worst thing was there was no shade. It was just rolling fields for miles around. We were toiling, floundering amid farmland. The land was seldom flat.

In an attempt to take our minds off the increased heat and effort, we had a discussion about the gears on our new bikes and how best to use them, given that we'd loads of them. I hadn't really got the hang of mine so far, I had to admit. It wasn't as simple as the Grifter XL with its choice of three gears. It was way more complicated than that.

'What are you on just now?' asked Stewart. I looked at the numbers by my left and right handle grips.

'Um, a two and a four,' I said. Honestly, I hadn't a clue.

My brother reckoned I should be focusing on the numbers on the right, switching between them more. I decided to make those my priority and see if that made any of this any easier.

We cycled past fields of vivid green beneath one of the bluest skies I've ever seen. We passed farm after farm after farm. At one point I got really confused, thinking we'd passed the same farm twice.

'Can't have done,' said Stewart.

'Nah, it's impossible.'

It was impossible. We'd been on the same road since the castle but it didn't stop me wondering.

As well as the mind–melt of identical farms, there were the ripe farmyard smells to contend with.

'Jesus,' said Stewart.

Rural Aberdeenshire reeked.

Neither of us had the nose for this. We were coastal boys, not country boys.

'Who to blame?' asked Stewart, 'The cows, the sheep or the pigs?'

'The cows, surely.'

'I think I saw a goat back there.'

'You did?'

'Aye, do goats look like llamas?'

'Goats look like goats, Stewart.'

'It was a big goat with a long neck.'

'It was a llama then.'

It was our very own version of *Animal Farm*: two wheels good, four legs goat.

The fields that didn't have animals were filled with rapeseed, bright yellow to the point of being difficult to look at, just like the sun.

Then we hit a long but gradual climb, hemmed in on either

side by tall hedges that ran the length of the hill. It was as if we'd entered a maze, albeit one with no corners and the only way out being to reach the top of the hill. The hedge on the right side of the road offered a few inches of shade. So we made the most of it by cycling tight to the hedge. There was no traffic on this back road and if a car were to come, we'd spot it a mile off.

Near the brow of the hill, we switched to the left and back into the sunshine, just to be on the safe side. A single wind turbine in a field beyond the hedge shot into the sky. I wished it could cool us down.

'I've not had this much sun since Australia,' said Stewart.

The latest summit brought the reward we were looking for, a giddy descent that still didn't seem as long as the climb we'd just made. Still, we got to freewheel for a bit, even if it was something of a downhill dodge with flies smacking us in the face.

'Ow …' said my brother, racing in front of me. 'Ow …'

He duly swallowed his third fly of the day and, upon announcing it, swallowed his fourth.

'Keep your mouth shut!' I cried and promptly swallowed one myself.

The only sound other than ourselves was the constant call of crows. We passed a woman in wellies out walking a pair of Border Collies. Shortly after that, we were overtaken by a tractor.

My brother, now cycling behind me, said he was starting to see some evidence of definition in my legs. My calf muscles were showing. Apparently when we'd left Hopeman, I'd shown nothing – and no wonder. Now though, I was starting to show some benefit from my time on the road.

Yes, I thought, new muscles! I supposed they would help with the pedalling.

Then I had another breakthrough. For the past half-hour, I'd been experimenting with my gears and now seemed to have figured them out.

'I think I'm getting the hang of these gears!' I shouted.

'Good,' said Stewart. 'It's only taken you 70-odd miles.'

We reached the village of Cuminestown and it was good to see buildings that weren't farms. One of the first was a pub. We didn't go in, but we did stand round the back of the pub for five minutes, grabbing some welcome shade and scoffing a banana among the broken glass and fag ends. We then got back on our bikes and proceeded to cycle through Cuminestown – and did it not feel like the longest village ever.

'This must be the longest village ever!' I said.

'No,' said Stewart. 'That's New Pitsligo.'

How could he possibly know that?

Whether Cuminestown or New Pitsligo was in the record books for being the longest village in existence, it took us an absolute age to reach the end of Cuminestown. First, recurring farms. Now villages that never ended. Except that it just had. Welcome to the countryside again.

'I flipping hate the countryside,' I said, getting it off my chest.

'Me too,' said Stewart.

Take that, countryside.

The question was, though, could we take it? We were at the mercy of a blazing sun directly overhead and had nowhere to hide. I tried to console myself with the thought that later on we'd be cycling in the early evening sunshine and it would be more pleasant than this. But that was some time away.

I knew that the combination of the high temperature and my low level of fitness was taking its toll, but I didn't want to think about it too much. If I was struggling now, what sort of state would I be in come an hour's time?

After a seriously unpleasant stint in the saddle, we came to the village of Maud, which sounded like it had been named after someone's auntie. Maud had a shop which we stumbled into to grab some life-renewing supplies.

A bag of bananas sat on a shelf, the only problem being that the bag contained ten bananas. We didn't need ten bananas. If we picked up that bag, we'd have to eat half a dozen bananas now and fit the rest in our bags. I couldn't stomach eating three bananas on the spot, or, worse, chucking some of them away. That would be a waste of bananas. This banana dilemma was making my head hurt, or maybe my head just hurt.

'Too many bananas can kill you,' said Stewart.

'Really?'

My brother started telling me about the amount of potassium in bananas and how too much potassium wasn't good for you.

'Of course, you'd have to eat a fair amount of bananas before you got really ill,' said my brother the banana expert.

'We're about to buy a big bag of bananas, Stewart.'

'Best be on the safe side then.'

We shunned the bananas and picked up some apples and Mars bars plus a humongous bottle of water.

Having paid for our bounty, we found the only shade in town by the door of the Maud FC Social Club (obligatory Tennent's logo on the wall) across the street. As we slumped to the ground, in hiding from the big orange thing in the sky that was making our lives hell, my brother pointed out the scattering of crisps on the road.

'Are those Discos?' he asked.

'They do look like Discos,' I said.

'I haven't seen Discos in years.'

This sparked a conversation about the favourite crisps of our childhood, culminating in our joint praise of salt and vinegar Skydivers.

There wasn't much to keep us in Maud apart from this rare spot of shade and we couldn't be banging on about crisps all day. So we did what we had to do and climbed back on the Green

Lantern and White Knight with the intention of making the Granite City before nightfall.

Aberdeen was bloody miles away.

Meanwhile we passed signs for Denbrae … Greenbrae … South Greenbrae … just about every sign for some hamlet or a farm had the word brae in it. It was either that or hill. Oh look, here came Middlehill now. I hoped to God there wasn't a Massivehill.

As we pedalled past our umpteenth farm, I had a brief conversation with a farmer standing by his gate.

Farmer: 'Hot?'

Me (gasping): 'Aye.'

Talking was proving difficult.

Earlier on in the day, when everything had been more rosy and less painful, I'd actually turned round and said to my brother: 'I'm quite good on a bike'. That comment was coming back to haunt me now, biting me in the sore backside with a vengeance. This was utter agony.

I saw a sign for Tolquhon Castle, but couldn't give a toss about castles any more. All I wanted was a dark room and a cold drink. We found this before we passed out, in a place called Tarves which neither of us was entirely sure how to pronounce.

We parked our bikes outside a pub and ducked in to order two half-pints of beer and two pints of water.

No sooner had we sat down than a ghastly smell engulfed us. Someone in the bar had just let themselves down badly by letting off an almighty stinker and it certainly wasn't one of us. Stewart and I scanned the bar, trying to pick out the culprit. There were six punters, three of whom could be discounted because they were sitting too far away.

Then one man, sitting nearby, rose from his stool and left.

'It was him,' said Stewart.

'Yep, definitely him,' I agreed.

'His parting gift.'

'Parting guff, more like.'

Mercifully the foul odour cleared and we were able to enjoy the rest of our half-pints in peace.

As we got up to leave, one drinker asked where we were cycling to, given that we were dressed head to toe in cycling gear and had faces like beetroot.

'Aberdeen,' Stewart told him.

The man grinned and raised his glass. 'I'll be thinking aboot ye when I'm having my next pint!'

I wanted to throw my bike helmet at the man but, to be fair, I might have said the same thing had I been in his shoes and on that bar stool.

Before we left Tarves, I dug out the route map to check on our progress.

'We're on a new page!' I cried.

This was a big deal. Each fold of the map had a different section of the route. We'd moved on to the next section. Psychologically, this was huge. It showed progress. Slow progress, sure, but I was taking any positives I could get right now.

Shortly afterwards, we passed a sign for Cauldhame. I couldn't think of a less warming name for a place. Well they wouldn't be cold today, that was for sure.

It wasn't long before we reached the village of Udny Green, which was as idyllic as it sounded. A few people were lazing about on the village green, which looked the perfect spot for a picnic only we hadn't thought to bring a hamper. All I had left in my bag was a Mars bar, which might well have melted by now. Even adding my brother's remaining Mars bar, we were still a few sandwiches short of a picnic.

We left behind the beauty of Udny Green and the hills kept coming, one after another after another. Finally we came to the hill that broke me.

My legs were killing me. I was wilting in this unrelenting heat and the hill itself was daunting and never-ending. One minute I felt terrible, the next I felt terrified. There was no shade, no let-up, no rest for the weary. I got halfway up and got off. Cursing the hill, the incessant sun and my own weakness, I ended up pushing the Green Lantern to the top.

I was disappointed in myself, but I could never have managed it. What made it worse perhaps was seeing my brother cycling ahead of me. Good for him, but it didn't help. This was the lowest point yet, at a high point in the awful Aberdeenshire countryside.

How many more hills were there between here and Aberdeen? Was I going to get off and push every time? And what about tomorrow and the day after that? Would I get any better at this – or, when we reached Aberdeen, should I just take the train back to Elgin and admit defeat?

Really, I hadn't treated this trip with the seriousness it deserved. My brother had come prepared with plenty of miles under his belt, whereas I had nothing and my tank was empty. I'd been found out. I was all talk.

I think it was round about then that I had a proper chat with myself. I tried to address my difficulties. That hill had been beyond me, in my present state, but I couldn't be making a habit of it, getting off my bike, however badly I felt. Because that would be the end of it.

There were two parts to this: the physical demands and the mental strain. I had to somehow condition myself mentally, without making myself ill in this heat.

Getting off the bike was giving up. If I kept getting off the bike, we'd never make Aberdeen. Even if I had no strength left, I needed to be stronger. What was left? I must have something, I thought. This couldn't be it. I couldn't allow it to be it.

Here came another big hill. This one looked even longer than the one I'd failed on.

I took a swig of water and cut out the negative thoughts. I focused on the top of the hill. There was a tree there, and that meant shade. I was going to stay on this bike and, when I got to the top of that hill, I was going to sit down under that tree and take in the coolness of the shade.

There was Stewart ahead of me, follow his example. Show your brother you can do this and prove that you are not a big liability on this bike trip that you suggested in the first place.

I buckled down. It didn't matter how slowly I went. Even if I was barely moving, I had to keep moving. I had all these gears, I needed to use them. I stood up, I sat down, pedalling in short bursts and pausing for quick breathers before picking it up again. I varied it, I did what I could. Gripping the handlebars, I stared at the tree at the top of the hill. In time, it got closer. I found a gear that worked for me, one I could live with. And I got there.

It was the one hill I shouldn't have been able to climb due to its size and the precedent I'd set by giving up on the hill before. But here I was and my brother was waiting for me. I could look him in the eye and not be the one who'd failed and had to push. I sat down under the tree and enjoyed the reward, Stewart sitting down next to me. Neither of us said anything.

I still felt broken by the sun and the hills, but the important thing was that I'd not let a pattern of failure develop. I was not going to push my bike any more today. Once I got on, I was staying on.

'Flipping hills,' said Stewart.

He was wishing for an end to them too, but they just kept coming until we eventually crawled into the next town of New-machar. I'd no idea what time it was and didn't want to look.

Hungry and thirsty, we cycled through the town until we found a shop and picked up some sandwiches and pasta salads. We ate them outside in the street. In finding our way to a shop, we'd come off the cycle route. Neither of us was sure of the quickest way to get back on it and the route map wasn't any help because it didn't show Newmachar in any great detail.

We asked a man coming out of the shop and he turned out to be the worst person in the world at giving directions. It wasn't that he was unhelpful, but that he told us too much. He'd begin describing the best way out of town towards Aberdeen and then start telling us about local landmarks and history. But now that we'd asked him, we had to wait there listening to him.

He hadn't really given us any directions yet. When he did give us some he took them back and changed his mind and suggested a better way for us to get back on track. We nodded patiently and listened. My God, this was taking ages. Finally he settled on what he felt was the best route out of Newmachar and back on the road we'd been on. We thanked him and pedalled away before he changed his mind again and called us back.

Safely out of Newmachar and back on the cycle route, we found ourselves riding on an old railway line. The man at the shop had told us all about it. It was the Newmachar Incline. Incline suggests up, but the Newmachar Incline was good news for us because the line ran uphill to Newmachar from Aberdeen. So for us, it was simply a matter of going downhill, pretty much all the way.

We hardly had to pedal at all and were able to freewheel for great stretches. My goodness, we deserved this. We flew past a man sitting on a bench, reading a book. His dog set off after us and gave chase for a few hundred yards before giving up.

Cycling the Newmachar Incline was a bit like walking on one of those airport travelators. With very little effort, you could move at a fair pace. Feeling a coolish breeze in my face, the effect of the Newmachar Incline was close to hypnotic. Either that or I had grown delirious again. Probably I had because now, in my head, I was pretending to be a train. I did everything but shout 'Choo-Choo!'

But my fantasy train journey was turning bad. Due to my earlier hill exertions, I was in some amount of pain. The pleasure of the Newmachar Incline was being taken away from me, just when I was starting to enjoy it.

It was payback time. My body was exacting its revenge on me for putting it through the mill. I found myself shivering in the heat. I also had stomach cramp. I never get stomach cramp. Feeling like I was about to be sick, I held on grimly for the most joyless freewheel of my life. A vacant passenger, I was like a slumped and injured cowboy on a galloping horse.

The shivering, the pains, the nausea all subsided after a while and then, after several miles of descent, we encountered, of all things, an uphill. But there was much to be gained by climbing it, since at the crest of the hill we caught our first sight of the sea since we'd left Banff that morning. We could also see Aberdeen – though it didn't look nearly as close as we'd have liked it to be.

Still, it was pretty much downhill all the way again to the Aberdeen suburb of Dyce.

My plan, when we got to Aberdeen, was to head straight for King's College in Old Aberdeen, where I'd studied at university. Actually, the plan was to head for the Machar, the pub next to King's College. After a pint in the Machar and the sight of King's College, we'd cycle the short distance to the house of our friend Brian, who was putting us up for the night.

Going to my old university stomping ground before Brian's involved more cycling, which we really didn't need at this late stage, but despite that and near total exhaustion, it's what I wanted to do. I wanted my pint in the Machar and to see King's College more than anything right now.

It might be that I was trying to link up with my younger self, the nineteen-year-old version of me. If that were indeed possible, my younger self would likely demand to know what the hell I was doing.

It wasn't my younger self I had to worry about right now as we trundled into the city at the back of eight. It was the drunk Aberdonian in front of us, doing some epic zigzagging on the broad pavement that was for cyclists and pedestrians and pissed blokes staggering home. He was all over the place. We gave him fair warning of our approach by ringing our bells, but that didn't work. So we slowed down and swerved past him. He didn't notice us. But we noticed you, Aberdeen Man. Your drunk-walking was the best drunk-walking we'd ever seen. We hoped he didn't get run over.

It was a relief that there was provision for cycling on the pavement because the traffic was getting hectic. We were happier when our route took us into the peace of Seaton Park. I used to walk through Seaton Park on my way to my morning lectures, when I didn't sleep in for them.

Emerging from the park we rattled down the cobbled street past St Machar's Cathedral. It was a bumpy ride, but I was coasting along on the excitement of being nearly there and knowing we'd survived this day.

As we neared the Machar, we passed a few students wandering about looking like students. I'd been building up the Machar for my brother – 'it's a cracking boozer' – but when we got there, it was shut.

'Bugger,' I said.

Talk about an anticlimax.

'What do we do now?' asked Stewart.

'Come on,' I said.

My brother followed me further down the cobbled street to King's College and we threw our bikes on the grass. We then lay down, using our backpacks as makeshift pillows. I stared up at the crown tower and the blue sky above it, then shut my eyes. This felt so good, even though my body was aching and my head was throbbing.

'Bloody hell,' said Stewart.

He'd said it. We'd pushed ourselves to the limit for 70 miles in the searing heat. In fact, we had gone beyond the limit. I had no idea how we'd managed those last 30 miles, but here we were.

After stretching out for ten blissful minutes, we picked ourselves up and cycled over to Brian's house.

'I can't believe you let Stewart cycle without stabilisers,' were Brian's first words when we got there. 'How did you get on?' he then asked, though he needn't have, since our faces told the full story.

'You look ill,' said Brian, directing his observation at me.

'I am ill,' I managed.

'What have you been up to?' my brother asked Brian.

'I've been doing bugger-all, all day,' he smiled. 'Reading the papers.'

'Just rub it in,' I groaned.

Brian was nice to us after that. He was the perfect host, feeding us a mountain of pasta, tons of mussels, hunks of bread and glasses of chilled white wine. I'd never had such an appetite and Stewart didn't hold back either. We ate until we could eat no more.

'Pudding?' asked Brian.

Both of us nodded.

Post-pudding, we sat on Brian's couch and let whatever was on the telly wash over us. Though we did pay more attention when the weather forecast came on. It looked promising too.

'Yes!' said Stewart. 'Cloud and northerly wind!'

Good news for sure. We were cycling south the next day.

'Just hold your jackets up behind you and you'll fly there,' said Brian helpfully.

'It's going to be a lovely cycle tomorrow,' I said, getting way ahead of myself and quite forgetting the trauma we'd just been through.

'I don't believe a word you say,' said Stewart.

'Where are you heading tomorrow?' asked Brian, filling up our empty wine glasses.

'Montrose,' said Stewart.

'It's south, so it's downhill,' I said.

'You sure about that?' asked Brian.

Chapter 3

East coast push for a Southside Shuffle

Day 3 – Aberdeen to Montrose

The morning after the day before, and my first discovery was that at least I could move. My limbs were stiff for sure, but there was a possibility I could climb on a bike again.

My brother was sitting in Brian's living room checking out today's route on the map.

'Flip,' he said.

'What?' I asked. 'What is it?'

'It's hilly.'

'Is it?'

'Up, down. Up, down. Up, down.'

'Okay, I get your point.'

He was making a daily habit of this. I was going to have to hide those maps from him.

'Shall we get going then?' I suggested. There was no rest for the bike freaks.

We scoffed some porridge; then Brian, who appeared to be on a bit of a health kick, handed us some protein bars and a bag of weird berries – I think they were Japanese – which he claimed would do us no end of good. I was willing to take any advantage I could get, real or imaginary.

We said farewell to Brian, thanking him for his hospitality and weird berries, and then hit the cobbled streets of Old Aberdeen again, which was a shock to the system and the backside.

As we rattled along College Bounds, students were making their way to their morning classes. That had been me twenty years ago, when I could be bothered to get up for my morning classes. I often found it easier to sleep in and get notes from a classmate who hadn't slept in. The amount of sleep I needed as a student was insane. As a father of two young children, I don't get much sleep at all nowadays. I hadn't slept very well last night at Brian's. My body was still angry with me. But I'd done slightly better than the first night in Banff.

We dropped a few gears and successfully took the Khyber Pass, the Khyber Pass being an Indian takeaway at the top of a hill in Old Aberdeen. It had been there since my student days.

Reaching the city centre, we passed the old university union, now closed sadly. It was the only place to be seen and get drunk in, in my day, and was partly responsible for me skipping those morning classes.

And now we were cycling past the Gotham City-esque Marischal College, where I graduated. I remember standing with my proud parents in the quadrangle in the pissing rain, thinking it was handy I was wearing a mortarboard. My other recollection of graduation day was not being able to recognise half my classmates as we'd all had graduation haircuts. Even the guys who'd spent four years with hair down to their arses had got it chopped so Mam could hang a nice clean-cut graduation photo in the living room. It was a shame really.

Marischal College stands on Broad Street, the windiest street known to man. The wind seems to shoot straight up from the harbour. I've never known Broad Street not to be windy. My brother and I were getting knocked about now.

'It's windy,' said Stewart.

'It's Broad Street,' I explained to him.

We crossed Union Street, managing not to get knocked down by one of a dozen buses. Then we braved our way down Market

Street and negotiated the maddest of junctions, chock-a-block with lorries heading to and from the harbour. I hadn't expected this to be pleasant, and it wasn't.

As we cycled along beside the harbour, I glanced over at some of the giant vessels. Among the less gigantic ones were the stand-by boats for the oil rigs. Dad had captained one of those – the *Grampian Pride* – in the years after he left the fishing. I'd been down here a few times to meet him for a pint at the end of his month-long trips. Cycling here now made me sad and I was sure Stewart was thinking of Dad too as we left the harbour behind us.

We wound our way up round a chunk of headland and stopped to look back on Aberdeen. We saw coloured cranes and granite spires. Marischal College was unmistakable, and another easy spot was the big wheel at Codona's fairground on the beachfront.

I gazed at the sea dotted with several tankers. Overhead, seagulls flew in a partly cloudy sky. I looked down on the mouth of the harbour to which Captain Sutherland used to return after a long hard month.

My thoughts were interrupted by my brother shouting: 'Dolphins!'

'Where?' I asked.

Stewart was pointing to an area of water near the harbour entrance and sure enough, there they were. Three of them, breaking the surface with elegance and then vanishing, only to appear once more. We watched them do this a few times and then they were gone.

'How about that, eh?' I said.

Stewart smiled. What a perfect start to the day, seeing dolphins for the first time, when we weren't even looking for them. Delighted with this surprise sighting, we turned our backs on Aberdeen and set our minds to the not inconsiderable task of cycling down the east coast.

It was an east coast scene all right, the blue sea and blue sky merging and becoming almost indistinguishable. A near imperceptible horizon, with nothing else to catch the eye. Scotland's west coast often draws the plaudits, but this was something.

We passed a house where someone seemed to have happened upon a unique combination of businesses. A hard-to-miss sign stated they sold fireworks and hot tubs. I wondered if you could get a deal on a hot tub if you bought fireworks, or vice versa. Bonfire Night's always freezing, but Bonfire Night in a hot tub …

Climbing a hill, I had a flashback to the dreadful day before, but I had come through that and decided it would stand me in good stead. Today could never be as bad as yesterday. It stood to reason I had become physically and mentally stronger as a result of it.

Another thing that struck me was that my brother had gone two days without hurting himself.

'I'll be fine, Gary,' he said.

'I know you will,' I said, trying to remain upbeat.

'My knee is a worry with the football, but it seems fine on a bike.'

Ah yes, there was the dodgy knee. My brother once tore his cruciate ligament playing football.

'That was the most annoying injury I've ever had,' he said.

'How did it happen again?'

'I was only clearing the ball, but I landed with all my weight on my right leg and felt a sharp pain. For weeks after that, my leg kept giving way and the pain would shoot up through my knee.'

He ended up having keyhole surgery.

'Just before I went under,' continued my brother, 'I said to the nurse that the injection hadn't worked. I didn't feel tired. She asked me to list all the ice cream flavours I'd ever made.'

'Eh?'

'I must have been telling her about me being an ice cream maker. So I started with raspberry then moved on to strawberry and mint. When I came round again in the recovery room, I sat bolt upright and shouted: "Fruits of the forest!"'

'You're joking,' I laughed.

'No.'

The upshot of the surgery was the surgeon telling my brother he'd been unable to properly mend his knee and that he should perhaps give up the football. Of course, he hasn't given up football. At least he sometimes goes in goals now, though. He's a good goalie, my brother. It's all those long hours of practice he had when we were kids.

'I've broken my right index finger too,' said Stewart, recounting another sore episode. 'At the hospital, I got high on the gas and the doctor yanked my finger back into place. I swear that finger is 5mm longer than my left index finger.'

'You're like E.T.'

'How do you know? You've never seen *E.T.*'

'I had an *E.T.* sticker book.'

'You had an *E.T.* sticker book but you never watched *E.T.*?'

'No.'

'I don't understand that.'

'Neither do I actually.'

'Mario wasn't happy when I walked into the ice cream factory with my arm in a sling,' said Stewart, getting back to the subject of the broken finger. 'First week of the summer and his ice cream maker wasn't fit to make any ice cream.'

Meanwhile we'd arrived in Portlethen, where we stopped at a shop to pick up some of the usual: bananas, Mars bars, water. I wondered if we ought to vary it a little, but it seemed to be working and I couldn't think of anything else to buy. Stewart had no suggestions for an alternative either. He was happy with our shop grabs.

Outside the shop, we unpeeled bananas and sipped water beside a bin, with fag ends at our feet. We always picked the most glamourous of locations for our pit stops.

Two old ladies had just bumped into each other at the door of the shop.

'Fine day,' said one to the other.

'It's going to rain at one o'clock,' said her friend.

My, that was specific. It seemed like a decent day to me. The clouds had mostly cleared (and there was none of that predicted northerly wind, alas). But she knew. Oh, she knew all right.

It got a little tricky leaving Portlethen. Looking at the map, the cycle route cut further inland and meandered north before heading south. Yet we identified another minor road that would take us due west for a bit and still allow us to rejoin the cycle route. This alternative would save us a few miles and several hills by the looks of it. It made sense.

The only problem was we had to cross the busy A90 to reach our road of choice. It was a hairy moment. In fact, we had to wait a good five minutes before we felt confident that the closest cars were far enough away for us to have the time to cross with our bikes, such was the speed of the traffic. We made it safely to the other side, but it was the least fun game of Frogger I've ever played.

After that it got less anxious as we muddled along a quiet road and eventually met up with the bike route. We then encountered the most baffling stretch of road yet. It really was something of a phenomenon. Both being under the impression that we were climbing gradually, looking at the road ahead, we found we didn't have to pedal at all. It was the slowest of freewheels, but surely we were going uphill? This road was playing tricks on us. Our surreal cycle lasted quite some time with neither of us able to make head or tail of it. In the end, I put it down to some type of optical illusion, the way the landscape was set around us, like Electric Brae in Ayrshire. Clearly we were going downhill – it just didn't look like it.

We made our final descent into Stonehaven on an obvious downhill that lasted a good couple of miles, which we managed to cover in about five minutes.

It was now time to go for a dip. Not in the North Sea (we weren't that brave) but at Stonehaven's open-air swimming pool, an Art Deco delight that's been around since the 1930s.

Stewart and I had swum there when we were kids, on one of our family camping holidays where Dad drove us all round Scotland in a hired caravanette. They were the best holidays, and I was so looking forward to taking to the pool again. What a way to refresh ourselves on our journey and, at the same time, revisit the source of some fond childhood memories. Before we had set off, I had reminded Stewart to pack a pair of swimming trunks for the pool at Stonehaven.

When we got there the pool wasn't quite open yet, but it would be in half an hour. All we could do was wait. We weren't missing out on this. So we went round to a café on the seafront and had coffee. It was pretty breezy sitting outside and I wondered how warm we'd be in an open-air pool on the north-east coast of Scotland.

By the time we got back to the pool, a queue had formed. We locked up our bikes and joined people of all ages going for a dook. I couldn't wait to put on my dookers. It's a fine word, 'dookers', far better than 'swimming trunks'. If I ever opened a swimwear shop, I would call it Dookers. I'd incorporate a pair of goggles in the signage, having them form the double 'o' in Dookers.

'What do you think of that, eh?' I asked Stewart, having informed him of my plans to open a swimwear shop called Dookers.

'I'd buy a pair,' said Stewart.

I then told him my other top business idea, which was to open a bar called Handlebar.

'It's a bike-themed bar, of course,' I explained.

'Sounds pretty cool,' said my brother.

I explained to him how the bar stools would be the seats of Choppers and the only music played would be by Kraftwerk (mainly their *Tour de France* album). Of course, there would be bike-based cocktails. Not with ball bearings in them, but with names like Tomahawk, Commando and Tuff Burner, the last of which might involve some fancy flaming effect.

'Would you drink there?' I asked.

'I'd never leave,' Stewart replied.

I really hoped no one else in the Stonehaven pool queue was listening enough to steal one or both of my recession-proof business ideas.

Once we'd got changed into our dookers, we got talking to a pool regular. The man said he had a bad knee which caused him trouble walking, but that he could swim with ease and cycling was also an escape. He explained how the local council looked after the pool during the summer months and that out of season it was maintained and cleaned by volunteers. 'It's an effort to keep it going,' he said, 'but it's worth it.'

Stewart and I stepped out of the changing room and into the cold air. I'd been warm enough on my bike, but standing here in my dookers I was freezing, even if the sun was out. The Costa del Stonehaven is not as scorchio as the Costa del Sol. Despite that, the brightly coloured bunting fluttering in the breeze over the pool made me feel like I was on a summer holiday in the 1980s.

'You go first,' said Stewart, staring at the water.

I gingerly lowered myself into the pool and was shocked. It was warm. I'd forgotten that it was heated seawater.

'You'd better get in here,' I said to my brother who was standing by the pool edge shivering.

It was a strange sensation being warm up to my neck but my head still feeling the chill of the cold coastal air. We spent twenty minutes in the pool, dipping underwater as often as we could. We then went and got changed back into our cycling gear. We did have some cycling to do before the day was through.

The two of us pedalled along by the harbour, which was full of sailing boats. It's a pretty town, Stonehaven, and we were just going to linger a little longer. An old schoolfriend had said we should pop in for a coffee if we were passing through and had the time.

Caroline was delighted to see us and made us super-strong espressos to heat us up after our swim and help us tackle the next leg of our journey. I almost choked on my coffee when she told us her husband had a Mongoose in the shed. I knew she meant Mongoose the bike and not mongoose the mongoose. That would have been cruel. As a boy, I was a big admirer of Mongoose BMXs.

We thanked Caroline for the coffees and she wished us all the best for the rest of our journey, pointing the way out of Stonehaven. It had been a bit of a flying visit, but I was glad we'd made the effort.

My brother and I faced an effort with the immediate climb out of town, but after that it levelled out and it wasn't long before we came to the cliff-top fortress of Dunnottar, one of the most breathtaking castles in the whole country.

In the seventeenth century, a small garrison held out for eight months at Dunnottar Castle against Cromwell's army, saving the Scottish crown jewels from destruction. In the early twenty-first century, my brother and I took pictures of each other pretending to do wheelies against the impressive backdrop of this castle that seems to rise out of the sea. Our position near the cliff edge was too precarious for us to attempt actual wheelies.

Done posing, we pedalled on, enjoying more of those east

coast sea views you could never tire of. Unlike with the west coast, there are no islands to catch your eye. It was just sea and sky, both now a matching grey, the effect still mesmerising. Everything looked limitless, yet at the same time it felt as if we were on the very edge of the world.

A while later, we reached Inverbervie.

We were standing outside the Bervie Chipper – the town's prize-winning chip shop – which wasn't open, when a car drew up.

'Is this a tour of chippies?' asked the driver.

It was only Caroline, who'd made us coffee less than an hour ago. She had her daughter with her. 'Cheerio again,' she laughed, and off she drove.

Over the road from the chippy there was an information board about the town. There must be more to Inverbervie than a chip shop, I thought. And, sure enough, there was.

Inverbervie was granted royal burgh status in 1341 by King David II in gratitude for hospitality shown to him and his queen, Johanna, earlier in the year when the ship bringing them back to Scotland – following a period of exile in France – was caught in a storm and forced to land on rocks near Inverbervie. I imagined the royal couple were probably treated to a fish supper.

My brother and I also learned that Hercules Linton, the designer of the *Cutty Sark*, was an Inverbervie boy. The creator of the famous tea clipper was born and died here, and was buried in the local churchyard.

After learning about Inverbervie, we followed a tiny road towards the fishing village of Gourdon.

I'd been told by someone with local knowledge that Gourdon had a cracking chippy – seems to be an east coast thing – worth seeking out. The afternoon was wearing on and we were both becoming ravenous. I wasn't sure about the wisdom of scoffing a fish supper when we still had some distance to cycle but, hey, we were hungry and nothing beats a good fish supper.

We followed a dizzyingly steep brae down to the harbour, enjoying the ride but at the same time thinking 'we've got to come back up here'. The chippy – Hornblowers – was set to open in fifteen minutes, so we went into the pub next door for a half pint. As committed cyclists, we tried to treat our bodies like temples. Everything gets worked off and according to my cycling friend Alasdair – he of the curlew incident – beer is full of minerals, and minerals are good for you.

The walls of the pub had lots of old photographs of Gourdon and details of the village's history. The fishermen of Gourdon were apparently among the first in the country to start long-line fishing from motor boats. Each line took hundreds of baited hooks. The men's wives and daughters did the baiting, after long hours spent finding the bait. While the men fished, the women baited the spare line for the next trip. Gourdon's harbour, like so many others on the east coast, would once have been full of fishing boats.

As I finished off my beer I read an account of a robbery that had taken place on these very premises one Sunday morning in 1787. The culprits made off with gold rings, silver spoons and seventeen shillings. They were caught and found to be responsible for a spate of break-ins in the area. Two men stood trial. They were found guilty and sentenced to be whipped through the streets of Aberdeen before being banished from Scotland for life.

'That's pretty harsh,' said Stewart.

'You're telling me.'

We were there at the door when the chippy opened and went straight to the counter to place our orders. I'm partial to a king rib or a white pudding, but there was no question: I was having a fish supper on this occasion. Stewart was similarly single-minded.

We took our fish suppers and tackled them next to the harbour while remaining vigilant of any gulls, especially ones of the black-headed variety. The fish suppers turned out to be everything they'd been cracked up to be. They were superb. You can measure the quality of a fish supper by the rate at which you scoff it. We wolfed ours down at an insane pace, which was maybe why we didn't have to fend off any gulls. We were that quick.

'Aw, that was good,' said Stewart, licking his fingers.

'Magic, eh?'

We allowed ourselves five minutes' fish supper recovery time – not nearly long enough – before facing the arduous climb up the brae. On the back of a fish supper, I don't think we fared too badly.

'I once ate a king rib supper in Hopeman then cycled to Elgin,' said Stewart, at the top of the brae.

'You mad bloke,' I replied. 'More like a cling rib supper … I don't suppose a fish supper will stop us getting to Montrose then?'

'Nae bother,' said Stewart, sounding as if he could go past Montrose all the way to Edinburgh.

We ploughed on, passing a couple of small settlements. The gardens of some of the houses were filled with chutes, trampolines and bikes, signs of childhoods being enjoyed to the full.

Too often for our liking, the route had us pedalling on a pavement beside the busyish A92. At one point, the long branches of trees almost crowded us off the pavement and caused us to have to duck to avoid them. Cycling ahead of Stewart, I gave him what I thought was fair warning of a branch I'd just narrowly avoided, but it turned out he didn't hear me. Seconds later, all I heard was a thwack and an 'ow'. At least he had his helmet on. Luckily this hazardous section of the route didn't last too long and we got away from the traffic and annoying trees as we switched to a quieter and more straightforward road.

Somewhere around St Cyrus, we came to a gate with a sign on it: Toads on the road.

'Toads on the road?' asked Stewart.

'That's what it says, brother. Seems there's toads on the road.' I opened the gate to let him through. 'After you, Stewart. Eyes on the road and don't hit a toad.'

I was just as nervous as he was. I didn't want to be running over a toad on my Green Lantern.

In the end, we didn't encounter any toads – perhaps the sign was a hoax, a strange hoax but nonetheless a hoax – and soon we found ourselves approaching the sprawling metropolis of Montrose.

On the outskirts of this Angus town, our stop for the night, we found ourselves cycling alongside a jogger. I say alongside, he was actually going faster than us, which didn't make us look very good. Eventually he paused for a breather and stopped showing us up.

'Show off,' muttered Stewart, not to the jogger but as an aside to me on the matter of Forrest Gump.

When we finally got to our Montrose B&B we had a lie-down, but not for too long because I had a night out planned.

'Where are we going?' asked Stewart.

'We're doing the Southside Shuffle.'

'The whit?'

'The Southside Shuffle – it's a pub crawl.'

'How many pubs?'

'There're quite a few, but we'll just do a couple. Call it a mini-shuffle, if you like.'

'Where did you hear about the Montrose Shuffle?'

'Southside Shuffle.'

'Aye, that.'

'From a friend of mine.'

My Montrosian friend Jade had told me all about the South-side Shuffle. It sounded like a dance and it was a dance of sorts, a dance round the pubs by the docks.

The other good thing about the Southside Shuffle – besides the name and the fact that pubs were involved – was that it crossed over with the Bamse Trail.

'The whit?' asked my brother, and not without reason.

'Bamse the dog.'

'Never heard of him.'

'He was a war-time hero, a Jack Russell in the Norwegian Navy.'

'He sounds like a character.'

So, to kick off our Southside Shuffle, I dragged my brother down to the harbourside so we could see the statue of Bamse. We found him easily enough, gazing into the distance and looking suitably heroic, while wearing a hat.

'1937–1944 Norwegian sea dog and World War II hero', read the inscription.

He didn't look anything like a Jack Russell.

'I thought you said he was a Jack Russell,' said Stewart, who would much rather have been in the pub by now than standing at the harbour staring at a statue of a St Bernard. 'Why did you think he was a Jack Russell?'

'I don't know,' was my honest answer. I'd no idea how I'd managed to confuse a St Bernard with a Jack Russell.

We read more about Bamse the St Bernard and his wartime heroics.

Bamse – Norwegian for 'teddy bear' – had been the dog of a captain in the Norwegian Navy. He sailed with his master on a minesweeper during the war. Bamse wore his own personalised tin helmet and would stand guard in the front gun tower during operations. The plucky St Bernard's presence lifted the crew's morale and Bamse became a mascot for the Norwegian Navy. He went on to attain legendary status in Montrose, where the captain happened to be stationed, and tales of Bamse's courage and kindness spread. In one act of canine heroism, he was said to have saved a young lieutenant who had been attacked by a man carrying a knife, pushing the assailant into the sea and dragging the lieutenant, who'd also toppled in, back to shore. Bamse was known to enter the dockside boozers of Montrose and break up fights between crewmates by putting his paws on their shoulders and leading them back to the ship before curfew.

He died on the dockside in Montrose and was buried with full military honours. Bamse's funeral was attended by hundreds of Norwegian sailors and Allied servicemen as well as many locals who had taken the dog to their hearts.

It just so happened that two of the pubs Bamse would visit were on the Southside Shuffle. So it seemed only right that they should be our chosen destinations for a mini-Southside Shuffle.

'I wonder if we'll bump into any ageing Norwegian sailors that Bamse forgot to bring back,' I said.

'Don't think that's very likely,' said Stewart.

The first pub we went to had cosy old leather seats and a real maritime feel to it, with pictures of boats on the wall and a ship's wheel. The only negative during our short time there was the big man at the bar – or the big wee man – abusing the barmaid to show off to his mates. He was half-joking, but half-bullying too. A pub can have a lot going for it, but it depends on who's in it when you happen to visit.

We moved on to the next pub. While the first one had initially looked welcoming, this was the sort of place you hesitated to enter. There was just this door and no way of knowing what it was like inside.

'Should we go in?' I asked Stewart.

'Well, we're here now.'

'After you, then …'

This second pub was a more spartan affair. There was no maritime memorabilia on the walls, just basic tables and chairs and a bar counter I didn't even notice until I turned round.

'It's your round, I got the last one,' said Stewart, keeping me right.

I ordered two pints. The barman never said a word as he poured them and handed them over. As we took our first sips, 'St Elmo's Fire' came on the jukebox. There was some serious darts action going on too.

The darts players were the only other punters in the place. The competition was fierce and the standard exceptionally high. None of them was having much trouble hitting treble 20 – but one bloke was doing it all the time. The electronic scoreboard only made it seem more like the World Darts Championship. My brother and I felt privileged to be watching such a top-level contest.

The bloke who was better than all the other blokes, who themselves were the best darts players I'd ever seen away from the telly, was wiping the floor with them. When he had beaten them all, they all shook hands.

'Well done,' said one of the master's crushed opponents.

The master then finished his pint, put on his coat and left the pub.

No sooner had he gone than the bloke who'd congratulated him turned to the others and said: 'Jammy bastard.'

Stewart and I looked at each other. We'd just seen what sport was.

We drained our drinks and headed back to the B&B, our mini-Southside Shuffle complete.

As we were walking up the road, a car cruised past with the windows rolled down and the driver blasting 'Eye of the Tiger'.

'Where are we? The '80s?' asked Stewart, who was just getting over 'St Elmo's Fire'.

Tuesday night in Montrose. I wouldn't have been anywhere else.

Chapter 4

Breaking off for a mince roll in Broughty Ferry

Day 4 – Montrose to St Andrews

Breakfast in Montrose in the wake of the Southside Shuffle wasn't all that dramatic. It was just me and my brother tucking into sausages, bacon, black pudding and anything else that we'd requested on our plates.

One of our fellow guests was on a firefighting course as part of his training for working on the oil rigs. He said he'd rather be out on a bike than fighting fires. So would we.

Stewart and I got on our bikes for the fourth day in a row and departed Montrose. I could feel the weight of the breakfast I'd just polished off. I also felt a twinge in my right knee. This was new and it worried me. It was a colder morning, I reasoned. I put the knee pain down to the weather as I didn't want to think of it being anything worse.

I had been looking forward to standing on Lunan Bay, one of the finest stretches of sand on the east coast, except we missed the turn off, after me talking it up. By the time I realised it, we had overshot the access to the bay by about a mile. We weren't going back. That would mean adding two miles to the day's journey when we'd enough miles to face.

We'd missed Lunan Bay but there was no way of missing Arbroath. The route took us through the town and for that I was glad. I like Arbroath. As we descended a big hill, a party of schoolkids was struggling to cycle up it in high-vis vests. The cheery teacher leading the group said hello. Not far behind him, one teenage boy, evidently having a hard time of it, groaned 'aw fuck'.

We snaked through the town and arrived at the harbour where we saw a sign saying 'Smokies, fresh off the barrel'. There was no escaping the smell of them either. I love Arbroath smokies but my gigantic breakfast was too recent a memory. As much as I liked the idea of scoffing a smokie in Arbroath, I'd have to pass. Stewart wasn't hankering after one either.

I was interested in the Signal Tower Museum though, and we were just passing it. I requested a stop and Stewart agreed to it. I'd always been fascinated by the Bell Rock Lighthouse. I was never going to get there – it was 11 miles out at sea on a treacherous semi-sunken reef – but I could still learn more about it at the shore-based signal tower that's now a splendid museum.

We had a wee wander around, checking out the exhibits. I couldn't get my head round the actual building of the lighthouse. To put one on a rock that far out at sea. It took two years to build, the foundation cut into the rock in 1809.

Every high tide, the rock was swamped by the sea to a depth of 12 feet. The labourers – the masons and blacksmiths – worked between tides for as long as they could before scrambling to support boats, making sure to pick up their tools before they were washed away. It was hard to imagine; I couldn't imagine it.

Once the tide lowered, they had to pump water from the foundations before they could carry on with their work. Lights were erected on the rock to allow work to continue when low tide occurred during darkness, which in winter time must have been frequently.

The tower was constructed with blocks of sandstone and granite and the lighthouse went fully operational in 1811. The engineer Robert Stevenson insisted a shore station be built in direct line of sight of the lighthouse. That's where my brother and I stood now.

'We've been here nearly half an hour, Gary.'

'Sure Stewart, just a minute.'

In the early years of the lighthouse, messages were conveyed between the rock and the shore via an intricate system. Both lighthouse and signal tower had tall metal poles with a copper ball attached that could be shifted up and down using a winding mechanism. Standard signals were passed, based on the position of the ball and the type of flag flown.

Supposedly if the wife of one of the lighthouse keepers was expecting a baby and it arrived while he was on duty, a pair of trousers or a dress was flown from the signal tower flagpole to let the new father know whether he had a son or daughter. It was a cool idea if it happened to be true.

Every fortnight, a boat would reach the rock with fresh supplies of food, water, oil, coal and spare parts. Although getting supplies – and replacement crew – onto the rock was difficult. When bad weather prevented a landing, the lighthouse keepers would eat dry crackers and canned beef, of which they had a three-month supply just in case.

The last thing I read about the Bell Rock Lighthouse, before we left, was a real eye-opener. They didn't have a toilet until 1964.

'What did they do before then?' asked Stewart.

'They must have –'

'Peed on the rock?'

'And –'

'Come on, let's go.'

There was no end to the delights of Arbroath. The famous Abbey where the Declaration of Arbroath was drafted – stipulating that 'all fish must be smoked' – wasn't quite on our

route, but Gayfield was. The home of Arbroath FC was just after
the Signal Tower Museum.

I'll never forget the day I'd gone to Gayfield to watch Arbroath
play football, or at least, to try to play football. That's no slight on
the players who battled admirably in near gale force conditions.
They should probably call it Galefield. It's the closest ground to
the sea in Britain and when the wind picks up, as it often does,
football becomes the most difficult sport there is. There are tales
of fish landing on the pitch at Arbroath and of a player being
knocked over by a wave while trying to take a corner kick. I don't
think for a minute that any of this is true, but I'll tell you what I
did see.

I saw corner flags bent horizontal and seagulls flying back-
wards. I saw a goalie take a goal kick and threaten his own goal.
I saw a ball boy fetch a bucket of sand for the goalie so he
could make a mound and place the ball better, because it kept
rolling away. I'd never witnessed a football match like it. It was
ridiculous. With ten minutes of the ninety remaining, the ref-
eree blew his whistle and abandoned the game. It was so bad
they couldn't play another ten minutes. It's the most memorable
football match I've ever been to and I can't even remember the
score or who Arbroath were playing.

Of course, the other thing about Arbroath is that they hold
the world record for the biggest win in football. In 1885, they
thumped Bon Accord 36–0 in a Scottish Cup match. One of the
Arbroath players scored four hat-tricks.

Arbroath lose more matches than they win these days, but for
their ground and their history they take some beating. One day
I'll write a book about them. I've already got the title anyway:
'When Smokies Sing'.

The title I was looking at now was PLEASURELAND, spelled
out in giant blue letters on the wall of the amusement arcade
bolted onto the end of Gayfield, making the football ground even

more unique. My brother and I thought we'd poke our noses into the arcade to see if they had Bubble Bobble or anything like that.

Arcades always bring back memories of the Hopeman café. For a period, I even worked the arcade machines when not making ice cream. I was in charge of the bag of change. When the gamers – my friends – wanted ten-pence pieces to play Bubble Bobble and Pac-Man, they came to me.

Away from the café, Stewart and I had a Sega Mega Drive in our bedroom. I think the first game we had was Altered Beast. We later lost countless hours to Sonic the Hedgehog. When we were really little, we had a ZX Spectrum with its rubber keys, all that palaver playing the cassette tape to load the game, the peculiar sounds and that stripy loading screen.

Manic Miner was my favourite Spectrum game, but I re-member my brother getting really excited one time when he discovered that the latest Shakin' Stevens album had a hidden Spectrum game at the end of the cassette.

Stewart was Shaky's biggest fan and had learned all the dance moves of the Welsh Elvis. He'd perform them at primary school discos, dressed head to toe in denim. The Shaky game on the Spectrum had you trying to avoid bats in a maze. It was a bit like Pacman, but not as good.

Pleasureland in Arbroath didn't have the Shaky game, Pac-Man or Bubble Bobble. It was all fruit machines that hadn't been switched on yet. We stood in the semi-darkness of an arcade that wasn't quite open and decided it was time to move on from our dreams of video games.

After Arbroath, we found ourselves back on a pavement alongside the A92. I didn't wish to be anywhere near this road. It detracted from the pleasure of cycling. It wasn't long though be-fore we were off it again, making our way along a much quieter road until we came to a gate. There was no toad-related warning but there was a sign saying: Please shut gate. Cows escape!

It struck me that 'Cows Escape!' would be a cracking title for a film. It needed to be done in the style of an old B-movie, a remake of a bovine Armageddon picture that was sadly never made.

Soon after the gate (which we shut to stop any cows escaping) we passed a group of young people – younger than us anyway. They looked like they'd been picking fruit in a field all morning. They looked exhausted. Suddenly, cycling round the country seemed less of a burden.

We came to Carnoustie and found ourselves cycling alongside the championship golf course. We spotted the burn where Frenchman Jean van de Velde came a cropper in the 1999 Open before Scotland's own Paul Lawrie went on to claim the Claret Jug.

My brother and I remember Lawrie playing Hopeman golf course, which he often did in his youth. I recall watching him tee off and thinking no one could hit a ball like that. Lawrie has played all over the world and in Ryder Cups, but his favourite par 3 is the twelfth hole at Hopeman. The Prieshach is hard to beat. It's Stewart's and my favourite golf hole too.

Back at Carnoustie, there was a queue of golfers waiting to tee off at the first and the course looked very busy indeed – the undeniable draw of an Open venue. The cycle path ran right down the length of the course and, at one point, we stopped to watch a group of golfers putt out.

'Go on, Stewart,' I whispered. 'Ring your bell.'

'You ring your bell,' my brother whispered back.

Neither of us rang our bells and Cyclists Enrage Golfers never became a reality.

It was a grey Carnoustie kind of day. I always associate Carnoustie with greyness. We could just make out the hazy Fife coastline on the other side of the Firth of Tay. We'd be in Fife soon enough, once we got to Dundee and crossed the Tay Road Bridge.

Having left the golf course behind, we found ourselves cycling next to an army firing range. I decided I'd rather still be cycling beside a golf course where the only flying objects were golf balls. We could hear guns going off and they didn't sound very far away. There were plenty of warning signs in case we thought it might be a clever idea to nip over the fence and into the firing range. One read:

> Danger Firing Range, Keep out When
> Warning Flags or Lights are Displayed

Fine, we'd do that. We'd keep out if flags or lights were displayed – but when would you ever want to go in?

Finally, we reached the safety of Broughty Ferry and the route took us right to Broughty Castle, so we thought we'd check it out quickly. A saltire flew from the top of the tower and we pushed our bikes up the cobbled ramp and through the castle gate.

Locking up our bikes, we climbed the spiral staircase to the top of the castle, though our bike legs didn't like it. Mine were demanding to know what I thought I was up to. You couldn't get a scone at Broughty Castle, but we didn't want one anyway. We climbed back down the steps – our knees yelling at us – and enjoyed the best part, riding out through the castle gate and down the ramp on our mechanical horses.

It was definitely time for lunch and luckily we'd the whole of Broughty Ferry's bustling main street to pick from. We tied our bikes to railings and went on the hunt. A butcher's window caught my attention. They were advertising steak burgers ('60p – Dundee's real discovery') but it wasn't the steak burgers I was after. They'd be sold raw. No, what I wanted was the 'mince roll for £1'.

My brother wasn't tempted by a mince roll and went off to

find a sandwich or something instead. We met back at the bikes, him with his baguette and me with my mince roll.

'What are you going to do with it?' asked Stewart.

'Eat it.'

'How?'

'With my hands.'

Stewart watched with a mixture of wonder and amusement as I bit into my mince roll, the gravy spilling out all over my hands and some of it dripping onto the pavement.

'Can't take you anywhere,' said Stewart, shaking his head.

I ignored him, taking another bite of my floury bap and getting a good mouthful of hot mince into the bargain. It was good butcher's mince, the kind we used to have at our granny's for dinner every Sunday, along with tatties and mealie pudding.

'Want some?' I asked, holding what was left of my mince roll to my brother's face.

'No, you're okay.'

'Fair enough.'

It was a mucky business all right and I think I lost half the mince, but my goodness it was tasty.

'You're not putting your bike gloves back on again, are you?' asked my brother, staring at my mince-coated hands.

'No, I'd better get washed first.'

I couldn't have my handlebars coated in mince. This wasn't a butcher's bike.

We ducked into the Fisherman's Tavern near the shore and I went to wash my hands while my brother ordered up two half-pints at the bar. No isotonic gels for us. The beer wasn't going to help us on the road; we just wanted it. It tasted so good, we wished we'd ordered pints of the stuff, but we both knew that way madness lay. No, we'd done the right thing ordering half-pints, even though the really right thing would have been two half-pints of orange juice.

I put my glass down on an old narrow table which had a ridge all the way round it. I recognised its type. It was a table from a fishing boat. Dad had one like this on the *Adonis*. The ridge was so the crockery didn't roll off the end of the table at sea. Now our beers were safe too. Not that the pub was suddenly going to pitch sideways. No, that would be after ten pints.

Fed and watered, we returned to our bikes and headed for Dundee. It proved a complicated approach to the City of Discovery, the route taking us through Dundee Port. We came to a gate where we were required to press a buzzer and look up at a security camera. Unsurprisingly, we were buzzed in. I couldn't think of anything less threatening to security than a pair of cyclists in full cycling gear.

But we still managed to fall on the wrong side of the port authority because, somewhere along the line, we took a wrong turn. Before we knew it, a car was racing towards us like something out of a film. I expected the driver to stick a flashing light on his roof, but he didn't. Instead, he came to a halt and gave us the stern look of someone in a position of (port) authority, pointing us firmly in the direction we were supposed to be heading. I had the sense that if we didn't obey him immediately and jump to it, we'd be interrogated in his office or something and I didn't wish for that to happen.

'Come on Stewart, hurry up,' I said.

'I'm hurrying,' said my brother.

Well that was frantic and it had us fairly flustered. Back on the straight and narrow, we managed to get to the other end of the port without further upsetting security or getting run over by one of the many lorries that were rumbling about. What a way to enter Dundee.

We found our way through the city centre to where we needed to be to get on the Tay Road Bridge, according to the route map. We came to a lift beneath the bridge that took pedestrians – and cyclists – up onto it. The only thing was that the lift was out of order and we couldn't see any other way of getting up there. We wondered what to do next as the traffic rumbled overhead.

Totally flummoxed, we thought for a minute we might have to swim the firth, until my brother wandered round the back of the lift and stumbled upon a craftily hidden set of steps. We hauled our bikes up a couple of flights and onto the bridge, where the path for cyclists and pedestrians ran between the two lanes of traffic. Gazing across the bridge, I noted there was a slight incline. At least there was very little in the way of wind.

We cycled along on the middle of the bridge with the cars to either side of us. It was very misty, the sea and sky slightly different shades of grey. I didn't once look back on Dundee – and neither did my brother. We'd nothing against the place. In fact, Stewart spent four happy years studying in the city and I used to enjoy visiting him. It was just that all the happy memories had been replaced by the more recent memory of Dad passing away in the city's hospital. Five years on, I still associate Dundee with the worst day of my life. I couldn't bring myself to look at it now. Maybe the feeling was more intense because my brother was here too and we were racing away from Dundee as fast as we could. We didn't say a word about it, but we were both thinking the same thing. I like to think that, in time, I'll get over it, that I'll come to enjoy Dundee again, because it is a fine city.

We came to the end of the bridge. I couldn't say I'd enjoyed it, but at least we now had both wheels planted firmly in Fife. We were making progress.

One thing was of concern though. Within the past hour, my right knee had started playing up again, just a little, but enough for me to be aware of it and think about it. Again, I put it down to the cold. When it had been sunny, my knee was fine. I hoped the soreness would go away. I didn't mention it to my brother.

Cycling towards Tayport, we passed a man sitting on a bench.

We said hello and he responded by saying 'aye, aye' and clapping, just the once, which was pretty unusual.

'What was that?' asked Stewart.

'We're in Fife,' was all I could come up with.

We ended up on a trail through Tentsmuir Forest and it proved very peaceful cycling among the trees. That peace was shattered when we reached Leuchars and heard an ear-splitting roar. It was a roar we both knew, but we'd never heard it that loud.

Having grown up a few miles from Lossiemouth, we were accustomed to Tornados flying over our house, but we'd never seen a fighter jet take off. We stopped our bikes to watch through the fence and were mesmerised by the white-orange glow from the engines and stunned by the sharp angle at which the jet took off. It was like a rocket.

After that impromptu airshow, we pressed on towards St Andrews. It wasn't long before we saw the first of many 'Danger: Golf In Progress' signs.

'Public using this path do so at their own risk,' said Stewart, reading another sign. 'Does that include us?'

'Of course,' I said. 'We're the public. What did you think we were, VIPs?'

'At least we've got our helmets on,' said Stewart.

'You could still get a golf ball off the arm. That would hurt.'

'Or one in the eye.'

'Let's hope not, eh?'

I was now fretting about my brother again. Statistically, I was pretty much safe. Statistically, he was a near certainty to get hit.

'Remember the time you swallowed your tongue?' I asked.

'Well, I'm not going to forget that, am I?' said Stewart.

My brother had gone to head the ball during a football match and got a knee in the temple.

'I was horizontal four feet off the ground and totally out of it,' recalled my brother.

'That sounds like levitating.'

'Aye, so I landed with a thud and swallowed my tongue. One of my teammates put me in the recovery position and pulled my tongue back out. My manager –'

'Same manager as when you did your knee?'

'Aye.'

'Poor guy, imagine having you in his team.'

'Aye, well he got me back to the changing room. Dougie came in too to check on me. When we were leaving the changing room I saw a game going on. I asked who was playing and Dougie said "us".'

'Did you not end up spending the night in hospital?'

'Aye, that's right. The guy opposite me got up out of his bed at one point, took one step and fell over, knocking his head off the radiator. He sat up and started laughing. He'd forgotten he'd had his leg amputated the day before.'

'Good God.'

My brother then started telling me about all the marks on his head, left over from past mishaps. Of course, there was the tiny scar that was the result of the argument he had with the bollard while riding his bike and eating a salad cream sandwich.

According to my brother though, the one next to it was from him and me once playing football with an orange in Granny's living room.

'Really?' I said. I honestly had no memory of this, but I suppose he was the one that got hurt and that was why he did.

'I was in goals,' said Stewart.

'Of course you were.'

'The goalposts were the legs of Granny's glass cabinet and you fired a shot towards the bottom corner.'

'I did?'

'Aye, and I dived and smacked my head off the cabinet.'

'Sorry about that.'

One final mark on my brother's head was the result of the most bloody injury he ever sustained.

He was playing football for Hopeman (of course) and the game was two minutes old, when my brother's first touch was also his last.

'I jumped to head the ball and was nutted by an ex-marine with a metal forehead.'

'Ouch.'

'I remember lying flat on my back watching the blood run onto the grass. I tried to move, but nothing was happening. My whole body was limp. My teammates stood over me and assured me everything would be okay. Then Dougie piped up: "Ooh-ya, I can see your skull." '

Dougie couldn't really see my brother's skull, I think. He was just making light of the situation, as best friends do.

'I was driven to hospital by one of my teammates,' Stewart went on. 'The interior of his brand new BMW took a bit of a splattering. So I got to the hospital and the nurse told me to take a seat. You should have seen the looks of fear on the faces of the other people in the waiting room. They were all avoiding eye contact as none of them wanted a blood-drenched madman sitting next to them.'

'What happened after that?'

'I got called through and ended up on the Batman set, the doctor complaining about not having the right tools. I thought I was going to end up looking like the Joker. Between the stitches and the glue it turned out okay.'

We managed to make it to the Home of Golf without my brother ending up in hospital. We even watched a group putt out at the Old Course's famous Road Hole and then tee off towards the clubhouse. Every one of them posed for a picture on the Swilcan Bridge.

After we'd checked into our St Andrews B&B, we walked

back down past the Road Hole and had supper in the Jigger Inn next to the Old Course Hotel. It's a well-known golf haunt, the Jigger Inn, but neither of us had ever been. Had there been a well-known cycling pub, we'd have gone there, but we were in St Andrews. Come to think of it, I didn't know of any well-known cycling pubs. It was high time I opened Handlebar.

The burger in the Jigger Inn was the most expensive burger I'd ever ordered, but it also turned out to be one of the best burgers I had ever eaten. My enjoyment of it wasn't even spoiled by the drunk American in full golf gear who sat down at the next table, leaned over and, pointing at my burger to the point of nearly touching it, yelled: 'Is it good?'

I told him it was and politely asked him about his round.

'Gee, well, tee shot at the first ...' he began and proceeded to shout at us for a good fifteen minutes.

Chapter 5

No man is an island unless he's in a hot tub

Day 5 – St Andrews to Edinburgh

We woke up in our St Andrews B&B with no aches or pains but a willingness to jump on our bikes and hit the road.

'I think we're getting the hang of this,' I said.

'Early days yet, Gary,' said my brother.

'No, I think this is it. I think we're going to cruise it.'

'Steady.'

Stewart's was the voice of reason and I was getting ahead of myself.

We sat down to breakfast and accepted anything that was a component in a cooked breakfast.

The thing was, I'd just weighed myself in the bathroom and I'd lost a bit since we'd left Hopeman, which just goes to show the benefits of cycling. You can eat what the hell you want.

Keen to get cracking, I devoured my breakfast at a ridiculous pace. I felt like I could pedal to Ecuador, never mind Edinburgh. I was itching to get going and pumped with confidence. It was the first morning I'd felt like that.

My only lingering worry was the memory of my knee hurting the previous day. Other than that, I'd gone from sore all over and daunted to saying 'bring it on'. Well, I didn't actually *say* 'bring it on', that would have been naff, but I had a sneaky feeling I was turning into a cyclist. I'd certainly had enough practice over the past few days.

We found our way out of St Andrews and hit the countryside in the morning drizzle. It was quite pleasant cycling in the light rain, feeling the spray on my legs. It was very refreshing, first thing.

We had cut inland and were heading towards the village of Ceres, another place we didn't know how to pronounce, not that it mattered. It all looked the same on a map or signpost.

The landscape grew more green and lush and mist clung to the hilltops as we pedalled past gurgling streams and small waterfalls. It was a nice stretch of road, all right. This was just about the happiest I had felt on a bike since I was a boy.

'I'm enjoying this,' I said.

'Glad to hear it,' said Stewart, cycling behind me, which was becoming the norm.

We rolled through the village of Freuchie, seeing the sign for the cricket club. I was well aware of Freuchie's cricket credentials. The village team was once crowned UK village champions at Lords. I remember it being in the papers at the time, this peculiar tale of a Scottish cricket team beating the English at their own game.

The rain was starting to fall more heavily now, more loudly too, but we remained remarkably dry thanks to the canopy of trees in this heavily wooded area. I realised we hadn't seen another soul for miles. All this was ours. Maybe everyone had gone abroad. It was just us and the occasional sheep scrambling out of our way.

It really was one of the finest sections of the cycle route so far. What few climbs we faced were gradual, yet there still seemed to be lots of scope for freewheeling. I could have cycled on this stretch all day, but then we wouldn't get very far. I wished the remainder of our trip might be like this, but I knew that would be far from the case.

We reached the historic town of Falkland at the foot of the

Lomond Hills (which thankfully we were going round) and I couldn't help but notice the palace. Falkland Palace was the country residence of the Stuart monarchs for 200 years. It was built by James IV in 1500, with James V later adding to it. I don't think any other Jameses were involved.

With the rain now bucketing down, we thought it a good time to hide with a coffee in the café opposite the palace. The man who served us was amazed we were cycling as far as Kinross, never mind Edinburgh. He gave us a free refill, perhaps out of sympathy.

'You picked the right day for it,' he said, looking out the window at the monsoon-like conditions. We couldn't complain, we'd had worse. I was mostly thinking of that second day in deepest, hottest Aberdeenshire.

By the time we got back on our bikes, the rain had relented a little. Leaving Falkland, we cycled through woodland where the Stuart kings used to hunt deer and wild boar. Another Stewart was riding by now, munching on a banana.

We soon heard gunshots echoing around us. It wasn't the descendants of the Stuart kings hunting cyclists, was it? It was hard to tell where the gunfire was coming from, but it sounded far enough away not to be of great concern.

A while later, we caught our first sight of Loch Leven from the top of a hill. As we made our descent towards the loch, we saw a few red deer. Commenting on the fine view of the loch, my brother added that we could maybe go canoeing. It was meant tongue in cheek. Stewart didn't really want to go canoeing, not with me at any rate.

The pair of us once went canoeing while on holiday in the Czech Republic and I turned a simple ride down a river into the most complicated thing imaginable. I just could not get to grips with the paddling and kept undermining the efforts of my exasperated brother. He'd paddle on the left of the canoe and

I'd paddle on the left. He'd switch to the right, so I'd paddle on the right. When we weren't going round in circles, we zigzagged from bank to bank. A trip that the canoe operator said should take one hour ended up taking more than two hours. It was the first and last time Stewart and I shared a canoe. I'm rubbish at canoeing.

'Hey,' I said as we cruised towards Loch Leven on our bikes. 'We should have done this trip on a tandem!'

'Maybe next time, eh?' said Stewart.

'At least with a tandem there's only one person in control of the steering.'

'Hmm,' said my brother. 'You'd probably still find some way of mucking it up, Gary.'

Something told me that we weren't going anywhere together on a tandem any time soon. Just like we weren't going canoeing in Loch Leven.

As we neared the lochside, I realised that in our rush and canoe chat we had somehow veered off the cycle route. Looking at the map, we should have taken a right further up the hill and headed for the town of Kinross that way.

'We were supposed to turn right, back up there,' I said.

'Thanks for telling me,' said Stewart.

We couldn't be bothered going halfway back up the hill and Kinross was next to Loch Leven anyway. We figured that if we followed the shore of the loch we'd be able to pick up the cycle route at the other side of Kinross. Seeing a man walking by, we stopped him anyway and sought reassurance.

'Aye, follow that roon there,' said the man pointing ahead with his walking stick at the path that hugged the shore. 'You cannae fail.'

That was a fine motto for the trip, that. You cannae fail. I decided to adopt it there and then.

We cycled along by the shore and eventually came to a jetty

where there was a boat that took tourists out to Lochleven Castle on an island in the middle of the loch.

'Fancy a wee boat ride?' I asked Stewart.

'Seriously?'

I asked the man on the boat when he was next leaving. He was heading out to the island in five minutes to bring some people back. The boat shuttled back and forth throughout the day so we could remain on the island for as little or as long as we liked.

'Right Stewart, boat trip,' I said. 'Lock up your bike.'

'You sure we've got time for this?'

'No, but we're going anyway.'

We paid a fiver each to board the boat. We were the only ones on it, apart from the man driving it, obviously. My brother and I sat up front, gazing out across the misty loch and the dark shape that was the island we were heading for. It was only a ten-minute boat trip and, as we got nearer, I could see the castle through the water-splattered front window of the boat.

Stewart and I were dropped off and a waiting group of four climbed aboard.

'I'll be back in half an hour, if you want back then,' said the man.

'Cheers,' we said.

Cool. We'd a whole island and a castle to ourselves. That hadn't been part of the plan when we'd woken up that morning. You never know how a day's going to pan out.

The island was tiny and very pretty. The castle ruins were impressive too. They took up much of the island. It was strange having all this to ourselves. We walked up to the castle and entered the large courtyard. Steps led up into the main tower so we climbed them.

Mary, Queen of Scots, spent time at Lochleven Castle. First as a guest, then as a prisoner. The tower we stood in was her prison during the most traumatic year of her life. She was taken to Lochleven Castle in June 1567. Not long after her arrival and imprisonment, she suffered the miscarriage of twins. She was then forced to abdicate her throne in favour of her infant son James VI. Within a year, Mary had escaped her island prison. She was smuggled out of the tower and onto a boat by the boat-keeper. Soon after, Mary was in exile in England.

We left the tower and walked back down the steps then wandered round the courtyard and walked back down to the jetty to await the return of the boat. Stewart started feeding the ducks.

'Och, no,' I said.

Now they wouldn't leave us alone.

The boat returned with a party of English tourists, some of them claiming they were being eaten alive by midges.

We weren't feeling it. We hadn't noticed any midges. Flies, but not midges. You would soon know if the midges were after you and there weren't any around here. Unless they were fussy midges and were only biting English tourists, which was always a possibility. The man driving the boat wound the tourists up a bit. No sooner had they set foot on the island when he started waving his arms and shouting: 'No, don't go in the castle! It's full of midges! Just get the boat back!'

They elected to stay. They were safe anyway.

When we got back to the shore, I phoned John the Chief. John had been the chief engineer on the *Grampian Pride*, the stand-by boat that Dad had skippered. Hence the name John the Chief. John lived in Kelty, which wasn't far from Loch Leven, though not exactly on our route. He told us we should drop by. 'I'll get the hot tub on for the two of you!' he said.

We had been summoned by John the Chief. We couldn't not go.

'Great stuff,' said John and he furnished me with directions.

When I came off the phone, I told Stewart about the hot tub.

He laughed. 'Well, at least we've got our dookers with us.'

We flew like the wind to Kelty. There was a fair amount of traffic on the road – more than we were used to – but we kept our heads down and knew it wouldn't be long before we got there. This detour was adding a few miles to our day, plus we'd just been pottering about on a loch for the best part of an hour, but we wanted to see John. I don't think I'd seen him since Dad's funeral.

We reached John's house and were greeted by him and his wife Linda. This man had spent more time with Dad in the last years of his life than any man. With all those long months they shared at sea, John knew everything about me and Stewart. It was good to see him. It was important that we'd made the effort.

There was the added bonus of the hot tub. We were treated like guests at a five-star spa resort and handed robes. My brother and I went to the bathroom to get changed into our dookers then ran back outside and climbed in the hot tub. It was total bliss, a treat for tired limbs on a cold day.

I closed my eyes and made sure I enjoyed every second of it, because, at some point, we were going to have to climb out of this hot tub and cycle to Edinburgh. What a thought.

Having soaked in the warmth for fifteen minutes, we reluctantly got out, put on our robes and walked into the kitchen, where we were treated to salmon sandwiches and coffee. First our private island with a castle, now all this.

'Magic sandwiches,' said Stewart, starting on his fifth one.

John asked about our trip and filled us in on his news. We didn't speak about Dad. It felt like it would have been hard. And we didn't have to. He was there in our minds. He was the reason we were here with John right now. We all knew what a good man Captain Sutherland had been, and we all missed him.

'Best of luck boys,' said John as we got ready to set off again. We shook hands with him and got a big hug from Linda. The side-trip to Kelty had been well worth it.

It was a shock to the system to be back in the saddle after that spot of luxury, but we buckled down and got on with it. Our next target was Dunfermline and we devoured those miles without much thinking about it. I'd definitely found a rhythm. It was like my legs were acting independently of me and cycling had become second nature. This boded well, if I could keep it up.

At the next junction, I almost mowed down three joggers, only seeing them at the last moment. I said sorry.

Once through Dunfermline, our next target was the Forth Road Bridge. We went the wrong way at one point and ended up on a scrub of wasteland. I checked the map and we retraced our pedalling until we were back on the right track. Before long, we found ourselves approaching the bridge. This was by far the most traffic we'd encountered yet, but we just went where we were supposed to go, following the signs for cyclists and pedestrians.

I'd been looking forward to crossing the Forth Road Bridge on a bike, and despite the overcast weather it proved quite a thrill. As we rode across the bridge, I kept looking off to the left, unable to take my eyes off the iconic Forth Rail Bridge. The view off to my right, down the Firth of Forth, was pretty amazing too, but it largely went ignored. As we neared the end of the bridge, the dolls' houses of South Queensferry down below began to grow into actual houses that people lived in.

Stewart told me about the time he'd crossed this bridge on a primary school trip to Edinburgh. He'd been ten at the time and the teacher had them get off the bus and walk across the bridge.

'Eh?' I said. 'That must have been some trek for a bunch of ten-year-olds.'

'Aye,' said Stewart. 'It took ages.'

We cycled through South Queensferry and began our final approach to the capital, our route mainly old railway lines that had been converted to cycle paths. Edinburgh wasn't far off now. It never seemed to get any nearer though. I kept thinking we were on the outskirts of the city, but I was always wrong. In my mind, Edinburgh was just a quick skip from South Queensferry, but it turned out to be more of a mini-marathon.

Why was this part of the day always the most difficult? Why had day become evening and we still weren't there yet?

'Maybe because we went on a boat trip and sat in a hot tub?' said Stewart.

'Hmm.'

We passed a couple pushing a buggy. The child said 'hiya!' and we said hello back. My wee boy had started saying 'hiya' a lot. I couldn't wait to hear Alexander say 'hiya' again.

Eventually we caught our first glimpse of Edinburgh. I made out the roof of Murrayfield stadium and, much further away, the big historic pile that is the Balmoral Hotel on Princes Street. I hadn't booked us into the Balmoral Hotel, but I had found us a budget hotel on Princes Street.

We were homing in on the finish line, for today at least, although the signs for the city centre were all over the place, in terms of telling us how many miles we had left. First it was four, the next minute it was two, then it was five. It kept going up and down like that and it was infuriating.

'These signs are crazy,' said Stewart.

They made no sense. I stopped paying any attention to them and just went on the assumption that we'd get there at some point.

At last, we found ourselves in the centre of Edinburgh. The place was a mess, with roadworks and tram works. There was even a sign that said 'trams only'. The capital was a long way off having those trams yet.

All the digging and blocked roads and diversions had us confused. We didn't know where to go. We got shouted off a pavement by a man in a suit. 'This is a pavement!' he yelled at us. 'It is for pedestrians!'

'I know, I know,' I said. Christ, give us a break. We've only cycled 60-odd miles to get here. Welcome to the capital.

We somehow fought our way onto Princes Street and found our hotel. It was directly opposite the castle. Normally I would have been wishing for a room with a view, but this time I couldn't have cared less. I just wanted a bed and hot water.

The hotel reception turned out to be on the first floor of the building and the only way up seemed to be via a lift at street level. The lift wasn't big enough for both of us and our bikes. I went first and had to stand my bike on its back wheel, front wheel in the air, in order to squeeze in. When the lift got to the first floor and the door pinged open, I basically wheelied my way into reception.

The receptionist didn't bat an eyelid. While I checked in, I kept an eye on the lift so as not to miss my brother arriving in style. It was fine for us to just wheel our bikes to our room, where we parked them next to the radiator. Bet they wouldn't allow this in the Balmoral Hotel, or maybe they would. I'll never know.

After quick showers, we took a walk down Princes Street. Everything appeared to be shut apart from one of the capital's many souvenir shops which was blasting bagpipe music into the street, so we popped in and had a look. This emporium of Ecosse was a blaze of tartan ... tartan hats, tartan scarfs, tartan shawls, tartan tablet. Okay, not tartan tablet, but regular tablet and tins of butterscotch and toffee and sticks of Edinburgh Castle rock.

It was all winter wear and sweeties. In Scotland, we like to wrap up for a trip to the dentist.

There was whisky, there were oatcakes, there was ...

'Stewart!'

'What?'

'Behold … the Great Wall of Shortbread!'

It truly was a wall, with tins of shortbread fingers and short-bread petticoat tails piled high. If you'd taken the roof off the shop, the Great Wall of Shortbread would have been visible from space.

'Remember when you used to make shortbread?' asked my brother.

'Yes,' I sighed.

As well as being a former ice cream maker, which was a lot of fun, I had once spent a summer working in a shortbread factory, which wasn't such a barrel of laughs. More burning hot trays of lava-like butter. It was hard work and dangerous for the fingers. Plus I had to wear a blue hairnet for hygiene reasons.

The worst thing about working in a shortbread factory was leaving it stinking of shortbread. You'd think shortbread wouldn't stink, but fresh shortbread clings to you like nothing else and quickly becomes stale. The minute you come into contact with anyone on the outside world who hasn't been making short-bread, well, you give off the most almighty whiff.

I'd get home from work and my brother would offer to wash me down with the garden hose.

We left the World of Tartan with its Great Wall of Shortbread and continued down Princes Street. A group of drunks was hanging around outside the tourist office. Their heated argu-ment looked to be escalating towards a punch-up.

My brother and I were dog-tired. We managed one pint then got some takeaway pizza and took it back to our room.

Before long, I was out like a light, enjoying the best night's sleep of the trip so far.

Chapter 6

Give me a barge any day

Day 6 – Edinburgh to Glasgow

I couldn't wait to get out of Edinburgh. Not that I had anything against the capital. I just wanted to get to Glasgow.

We made our way through Edinburgh's western suburbs and hooked up with the towpath of the Union Canal which would take us all the way to Falkirk where we would follow the Forth & Clyde Canal all the way to Glasgow. It was going to be a canal kind of day.

In my imagination, this meant a fairly leisurely day's cycling, perhaps even the easiest one yet. Of course, this turned out not to be the case.

The heavy rain had made the towpath muddy and the cobbled sections very slippery. Progress was tricky and, seeing as we were cycling right beside the water, reasonably stressful.

'How deep is the canal?' asked Stewart.

'I've no idea,' I said.

I'd no intention of finding out either.

Then there were the bloody aqueducts. Yes, it's a novel experience cycling along an aqueduct, high above a river or a motorway, but it's also pretty hairy. The path was at its narrowest on the aqueducts, with signs telling cyclists to dismount and no wonder. It was a tight spot, wheeling the Green Lantern and the White Knight single file beside the canal. One slip in this wet weather and it was goodbye bicycle. Then, if someone came the other way, one of you had to stop to let the other squeeze past.

Ready if you are: Acting like we know what we're doing as the hour of departure arrives.

Firth impression: The Moray coast in all its glory and not a Great Black-backed Gull in sight.

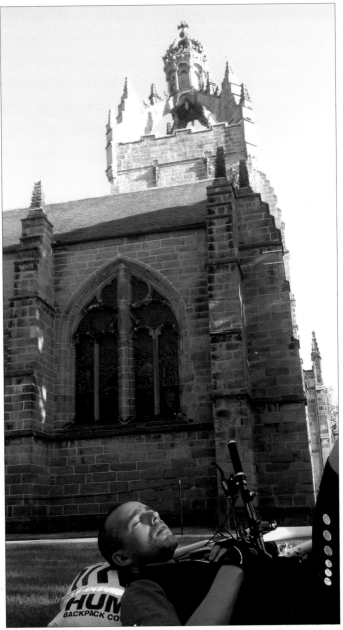
Eyes wide shut: Stewart crashes out in the shadow of King's College, Aberdeen.

Drinking in the scenery: Knocking back a beer at Loch Drunkie.

High and mighty: Ach, it wasn't that hard getting here.

Looking back: Halfway up our umpteenth hill in the Highlands.

A sense of place: No clue where I am or how I got this far. Stewart, any ideas?

You shall not pass: Too good an opportunity not to sit down.

Horns of a dilemma: How to cope with a Highland cow roadblock?

Sight for sore eyes: Strathmore reveals itself and stuns us into momentary silence.

Gimme shelter: Stewart makes himself at home.

Inn you go: A welcome pit stop at the one and only Crask.

Hello, Mam: Waving to Hopeman from Tarbat Ness.

Home and dry: Back on Dunbar Street with the Grifter XL and Tuff Burner.

We let a woman edge past us on an aqueduct. She asked if we were twins. It was a fair question for two brothers close in age and dressed so similarly.

We also had to take great care going under the many bridges that crossed over the canal. The bridges offered welcome cover from the rain, but the cobbles were damp and, again, there really wasn't much room. At the bridges we both felt scarily close to the water. One wrong move and we were most certainly in there.

What a dreich pain of a day this was. Nice weather for ducks, swans too. A man walked by with a brolly in one hand and a can of Tennent's in the other.

'It's wet the day, eh?' he said. Even with a brolly for protection, there was no way he was remaining dry this morning.

We stopped under another bridge for shelter. It really was bucketing down.

Struggling on, we caused what we thought was a heron ('it isn't a seagull', said Stewart helpfully) to take flight and flap its way up the canal. It was quite a sight seeing it glide along like that.

Then we saw our first barge of the day. Up front was a woman in a wheelchair, a nurse at her side. I later learned about the Seagull Trust and the canal cruises they provide for individuals with special needs.

We passed a few signs along the way promoting the use of the canal to cyclists. 'It's all on the level,' was the message. Well, yes it was. A level route was great, but the soggy and slippery conditions were making this a real struggle today. We really were getting bogged down – and here was me believing Edinburgh to Glasgow would be a breeze.

Overgrown bushes and overhanging trees were also a nuisance. We didn't want to be any nearer the canal than we already were. Smacking into branches and having water drip down your neck wasn't much fun.

It was all very well for the chirping birds, they could flap themselves dry. We were getting more and more drenched. It was a miserable experience and we tried to find comfort in whatever we could, like the occasional blossom on the towpath, which resembled confetti.

'It's like a wedding,' said Stewart.

Yes, cause for celebration. We were married to our bikes, but wanted a quick divorce from this flipping towpath.

Eventually we realised that we were going to have to come off it if we were to have any chance of getting to Glasgow. We were going nowhere fast and really needed to be on a road on a day like this. At the next opportunity we gave up on the canal dream that had become a nightmare and embraced tarmac. Although we were between Edinburgh and Glasgow, it wasn't a major road and the traffic wasn't too bad. We just wanted to get to Linlithgow and find somewhere to dry off and perhaps grab some lunch too.

Just to be sure we were on the right road, we asked two women puffing away at a bus stop. 'Aye, that way,' they said at the same time, pointing their fags in the direction we were heading.

When we got to Linlithgow, we found the nearest super-market. Looking like a pair of drowned rats, we trudged down the aisle towards the toilets, leaving a trail of mud. We changed into dry clothes, leaving ourselves with a bunch of wet clothes which we stuffed in carrier bags that were then squeezed inside our backpacks.

We then found a warm pub and had a bite to eat and the ob-ligatory half pint. The beer was hoppy, which was to our liking, but we were far from happy as we felt very far from Glasgow, which was the truth.

Despite the cosy nature of the pub, it was a struggle to warm up. This was about the most soaked and chilled to the bone I'd ever been. Stewart's teeth were chattering.

'Hey, Mr Chatterteeth!'

'It's nae funny.'

'No it isn't, is it?'

We reluctantly returned to our bikes and as we left Linlithgow – passing its stunning palace, which we'd no time for – a bunch of schoolboys gave us a cheer.

That's nice, I thought.

Then one of them cried: 'You can do it! You can do it!' in an American accent.

'They're taking the piss, aren't they?' I said.

'Yep,' said Stewart.

Within ten minutes of leaving Linlithgow, we had to stop and put on some sunscreen. The rain clouds had cleared and the sun was now beating down. It was the strangest of days.

Feeling more confident, we thought we should try out the canal again. Maybe it wouldn't be so bad in drier weather, plus I'd no real idea about getting to Glasgow by road and didn't fancy it.

'Should we give it a go?' I asked.

'Why not?' Stewart replied. 'We can always come off it again.'

We found our way back onto the canal towpath and were pleasantly surprised at what we found. The weather was helping, but the path also seemed more generous and firm than it had been on those early exasperating miles out of Edinburgh.

Soon we heard the roar of a motorbike up ahead of us. Then we saw them, a teenage boy riding the bike with his shirtless pal on the back, filming it all on his camera phone. They were racing back and forth, being watched by half a dozen of their menacing-looking mates in tracksuits.

I braced myself for some abuse as we went past, but they left us alone.

Not long after, we encountered an unexpected tunnel. Not only was it unexpected, it was also incredibly long. We peered into the darkness and saw the tiniest chink of light at the other end.

'Um, are we meant to go through this?' asked Stewart.

'Looks like it,' I said.

The towpath continued with the canal through the tunnel, which looked to be at least half a mile long. All that separated the damp cobbled path from the inky water was a flimsy looking wooden barrier. We were obviously going to have to push our bikes all the way.

'You go first,' said Stewart.

I wasn't sure about that, but recalled that in the cartoons of my childhood it was always the straggler at the back that got captured. Not that I wanted my wee brother to vanish or anything, and for me to have to go on an adventure and find him and rescue him from the clutches of an incompetent villain.

There was actually the dimmest of lights in the tunnel, though you wouldn't exactly call it floodlit. It was all very dank, the tunnel walls covered in moss. The creepiest aspect, besides just being in a long, dark tunnel, was looking over the fence into the murky water.

We pushed our bikes towards the light on our unwelcome tunnel adventure. It seemed to take forever, the tunnel exit never getting any bigger as we edged towards it. When I thought we'd gone halfway, I looked back to see that we had covered a quarter of the tunnel at best.

'Aw, man,' I sighed.

'Highlight of the day,' said Stewart.

When we eventually reached the end of the tunnel, we greeted the sight of the countryside like it was the best thing we'd ever seen.

'That was fun,' said Stewart. 'Fancy doing it again?'

I later found out that the tunnel was 600 metres long and also – from a friend who had grown up in the area – that a legendary monster pike was said to live there. If I'd known that, I'm not sure I'd have gone through with it.

The next phenomenon we encountered – and a far less claustrophobic one, at that – was the Falkirk Wheel, the world's only rotating boat lift and a triumph of engineering. We'd no cause to use it, seeing as we had come by bike and not boat, but it was still a cool thing to clap eyes on.

It was here that we left the Union Canal and joined the Forth & Clyde Canal. In their nineteenth-century heyday, both canals would have been busy with barges carrying cargoes of coal, stone and lime from Scotland's industrial heartland to its two major cities. The railways and the roads led to the decline of the canals but, in recent years, they have been restored for leisure purposes. After a bad start, we were now enjoying our canalside ride.

Before long, we were passing Bonnybridge, Scotland's UFO hotspot, known for being the scene of numerous unexplained sightings. My gaze shifted upwards, but all I could see in the sky were seagulls.

'Could be seagull-shaped UFOs,' said my brother.

'They're seagulls, Stewart.'

'Where was it you saw your UFO again?'

'On a train near Stirling.'

My brother wanted to hear the story again, even though he didn't believe a word of it.

I'd been on a train from Glasgow to Inverness. It was a beautiful morning, the sky the clearest blue, with not a cloud to be seen. I was reading the newspaper when the man sitting opposite me said: 'What's that?'

I looked up. He was looking out of the window, pointing upwards.

I looked and there was something in the sky. It was white, with a lattice-like pattern.

'It was a cloud,' said Stewart, interrupting my recounting of a story he had no faith in.

'No, it wasn't a cloud. It was something else.'

'A seagull?'

I ignored him and finished my story. Back on the train, my fellow passenger and I watched in silence as this white lattice-like structure rose fast at a sharp angle. This went on for about twenty seconds and then suddenly it disappeared. It didn't go behind a cloud, because there weren't any. It just vanished, like that.

I'd looked at the man and he'd looked at me. We both shrugged, him returning to his magazine and me getting back to my paper. We never said another word about it. My fellow UFO-spotter got off at Stirling and I carried on to Inverness.

'Are you sure it wasn't a smudge on the window?' asked Stewart.

'But we were looking at it from different angles,' I said.

'Hmm. What shape was it again?'

'It looked a bit like the Eiffel Tower.'

'The Eiffel Tower, eh?'

He didn't believe me. But I know what I saw, even if I didn't know what I saw.

I also saw a panther once on the outskirts of Perth, but that's another story.

We cycled beneath the M80 – the number of times I've been on that motorway, heading in and out of Glasgow, the city that had become home. It felt close now. We still had some miles to tackle, but the end of a day that got off to the worst possible start was in sight.

As we breezed along the towpath, we enjoyed the view of the Kilsyth hills. Ahead of us a couple was walking on the path. I was riding in front of my brother and wasn't able to warn them of our approach as I found that, somewhere along the line, a bit of my bike bell had broken off, the bit that made it ring.

I called out to the couple, but they didn't hear me. I tried again and this time they heard, shifting to the side to let us pass.

'Sorry,' I said. 'My bell's not working.'

'I've got the same problem, son,' said the man.

Everyone laughed, including the man's wife. I could tell we were close to Glasgow.

We soon came to Kirkintilloch, a 'Walkers are Welcome' town, according to the sign.

'What about cyclists?' I asked.

'Oh, they're banned,' said Stewart.

We didn't encounter any resistance in Kirkintilloch and stopped at a shop for one last Mars bar and banana for the road. We sat on a bench by the canal and ate them.

After that, we cycled on in the evening sunshine. It was beautiful by the canal now and I felt we'd earned it.

Nearer the city there were more pylons, then we passed the first tower blocks. A man walked by with a pit bull. Then another man passed on a bike and I couldn't help but notice that where his water bottle should be there was a can of Tennent's. When I looked back a minute later, he was off his bike and peeing in the canal.

There was then, though, the far nicer sight of a dad pushing a pram, his child smiling up at him.

We reached the locks at Maryhill and I knew I was nearly home. I'd cycled here from my house as part of my, ahem, training regime.

Stewart and I pushed on and pretty soon we were leaving the canal and cycling down the street to my house. I'd never been so glad to see my own front gate. We threw on a pile of washing and then jumped on the train to Partick. The plan was to have a quick beer then pick up a takeaway curry. The two of us were enjoying the reward of a pint when my friend Victor walked into the bar.

'How are you getting on?' asked Victor. 'You look tanned and toned, guys!'

'Thanks very much,' I said. I'd never been called tanned and toned in my life, and likely never would again.

'What are you on?' asked Victor.

'Oh no,' I said. 'We're just in for the one.'

Victor was having none of it. Impressed by our cycling efforts, he insisted on buying us a drink.

Ach well, we deserved it.

Chapter 7

Happy hour at Loch Drunkie

Day 7 – Glasgow to Callander

The sun had got his hat on and we had on our bike helmets for another day of canal action with a few lochs thrown in.

My brother and I were heading north towards Inverness on what Sustrans liked to call the Lochs & Glens route. I liked that it was lochs and glens and not lochs and mountains. It didn't sound nearly so bad.

Having cranked up the heating overnight, we had clean, dry bike gear, making us well laundered, smelling nice and raring to go. I shut the front gate, feeling as if I'd just opened it a moment ago. Home sweet home had been more like home swift home.

It was just under 20 miles to Balloch on the south shore of Loch Lomond. After that we were heading for the heart of the Trossachs, with the town of Callander being our stop for the night. We were talking 50 miles in total, which didn't seem that much, really.

Back on the canal towpath, the joggers were out in force. There were plenty of dog-walkers too and a few folk fishing. One or two men on the path looked to be running morning er-rands, but on closer inspection their carrier bags contained just cans of beer. What a start to the day that was.

At Clydebank, we pedalled past a moored boat billed as 'the world's first sail-thru fish and chip takeaway'. A few miles later, we came to a canalside bike shop. It was in a great spot, which they had made the most of by displaying their bikes by the water with the boats behind them.

We went in because I'd been meaning to pick up a spare inner tube. Stewart didn't have one either. We'd gone six days without any and didn't want to push our luck any further.

While the man in the bike shop sorted us out, Stewart and I couldn't help but admire the brand new BMX behind the counter. It looked a lot like a Tuff Burner.

'It's the boy's birthday,' said the man. 'He's picking it up today.'

Lucky boy, I thought. And the happiest boy for miles around soon.

We got back on the bikes and reached the end of our canal time. Now we were cycling alongside the River Clyde towards Dumbarton. Pedalling through the town, we caught a couple of glimpses of Dumbarton Castle atop the hard-to-miss Dumbarton Rock.

Leaving Dumbarton, we were now following the River Leven all the way to Loch Lomond. We were soon surrounded by marshland. I didn't expect it to get so swampy. It was like something out of *Gentle Ben*.

'Stewart, keep your eye out for bears,' I said.

'Bairns?'

'No, bears.'

Bears turned out to be the least of our problems. Or my problem. When a sharp pain shot down my right knee to my foot, I had to get off.

'Stewart, I have to stop.'

'Okay.'

It was the same knee in which I'd been feeling the occasional twinge, but this was far worse. I got off the Green Lantern and the minute I put my foot on the ground, the pain shot through my leg again.

'Ow,' I cried.

Stewart said nothing, not out of lack of sympathy but a lot of concern. I sat down on the grass. This wasn't good.

I gave it a minute and got up. Carefully, I put some weight on my leg and got the same deal – a red hot knee and spreading pain that made me want to shout and swear and quite possibly cry.

I sat down again.

'This isn't good,' I said.

'No,' said Stewart. He didn't know what to say and neither did I.

I began having dark thoughts, thoughts that I might not be able to complete the journey, that seven days into this fifteen-day bike ride round Scotland, it was all over. This was it.

I even wondered where the nearest hospital was and wondered if I should go there and get my knee checked. Could I do that and then we'd be okay?

I got up again, bracing myself for the same agony, but it didn't come. I walked towards my bike, felt a sharp twinge and stopped.

'Sorry Stewart, I need to sit down again.'

'Sure, take your time.'

The unsaid remained unsaid.

I stood up one more time, letting my left leg bear all the weight, and hopped over to a nearby information point for something to do. I read about the history of the area.

Scotland's first bleachfields were established around here. Back in the eighteenth century there were nine factories on this stretch of the River Leven, employing thousands of people. The local textile industry expanded from bleaching into printing and dyeing.

This was kind of taking my mind off my knee.

Then I read about Renton Football Club. We must be near Renton. They won the Scottish Cup in 1885 and again in 1888 when they went on to play English FA Cup winners West Bromwich Albion in a challenge match. Renton beat West Brom and declared themselves World Champions. How about that?

I slowly put some weight on my right leg and didn't get the reaction I feared. Then I very carefully hobbled over to my bike and tried to get on. It was a job, but I made it.

'I'm on,' I announced.

'Let's see how it goes,' said Stewart. 'It could be your cruciate.'

'Tell me it isn't.'

The mood was distinctly downbeat.

I started pedalling slowly. After a couple of revolutions, I felt the shooting pain from my right knee again as I pushed downwards with that leg. So I decided to pedal with just my left leg for a bit, as much as you can pedal with one leg. I knew I couldn't pedal round the country with one leg, but it was a start and better than sitting on the ground feeling sorry for myself.

How on earth was I going to cycle another 30 miles today? Was it even possible?

We were approaching Alexandria. That's Alexandria, East Dunbartonshire and not Alexandria, Egypt. I wondered if there was a hospital in Alexandria that I could go to and see about my knee. But what if they looked at it and told me I'd damaged it and that I couldn't be getting back on my bike again? Someone would end up taking the decision for me and that would be it.

I tried to pedal normally and, on the third or fourth push down on the bad leg, I felt the pain again. I wondered if I could position the leg at an angle, say, pushed my knee out a bit, if that might help. I tried that and went half a dozen revolutions without pain, while still applying pressure on that leg.

'You okay?' asked Stewart.

'I don't know, I need to watch.'

We weren't going anywhere fast.

'There's no hurry,' said Stewart. 'We can stop for lunch soon.'

I thought that even if we took our time and it took all day and well into the evening and we got to Callander before nightfall, that would be success. And after a hot bath and a good night's sleep, my leg might be fine in the morning and in the long run.

But what if I was doing untold damage to my knee just now, by being on the bike? Maybe I was properly knackering it. My mind was in a muddle. I just wanted everything to be right again. I had invested so much time and effort in this. We both had.

We reached Balloch with its pleasure boats and tourists drawn here for Loch Lomond. We once camped at Balloch on one of our family caravanette holidays. I recalled us having fish and chips.

Stewart and I went into the nearest pub and ordered our lunch and half pints of ale and glasses of water. I sank into a comfy armchair. The lights in the bar were turned down low and the room was cool in comparison to outside. I stretched out my legs and closed my eyes.

'How's the knee?' asked Stewart.

'Okay so far.'

How was it going to behave the rest of the day, I wondered. We had a long and no doubt difficult afternoon ahead of us.

'Whatever it is,' said Stewart, 'it could be you can build up the strength in your knee by pedalling carefully for a bit and the pain might go away.' He didn't sound entirely certain, but I was willing to give it a go more than I wanted to pack it in.

After lunch and the welcome rest, I raised myself from the armchair and walked out of the pub. I felt a twinge, but it wasn't the sharp pain. I then got on my bike and that's when it hurt. I'd raised the right leg over the bar first to get on. I was going to have to mount and dismount the other way. It was all about adapting, protecting my weakness and using that leg sparingly.

You can't really cycle using one leg sparingly, but that's all I had right then. I was still anxious, but I'd moved on from the despair of sitting on the grass near Renton.

On the way out of Balloch, a man walking a mean-looking dog saw us coming towards him slowly. I think he thought we were hesitating because of the dog, whereas the truth was I couldn't go any faster. In any case, he decided to reassure us.

'Don't worry,' said the man. 'He doesn't chase bikes.'

No, I thought, looking at the dog. He just chews them up and spits them out.

Edging back into the countryside, we set about tackling the first hill after lunch. It was also the first proper hill since I'd broken down an hour ago. A lot depended on this.

I used my new pedalling technique, if it could be called a technique. I continued to push down harder on my good left knee, leaving me less to do with the troublesome right. I kept the right knee jutted out at what seemed like the best angle for avoiding pain. And I worked my gears to my best advantage.

I also tried the tactic I'd employed that terrible second day in Aberdeenshire when the hills and heat had almost defeated me. I played out the battle in my mind. I told myself I could do it, that I had to or else the game was up. Imagining that the bike and I were one, I focused on the pure motion and told myself there was no sore knee. I blocked it out for the duration of the hill and made it to the top without too much pain.

'Well done,' said Stewart.

'Cheers,' I said. It felt like a major victory.

On the next climb, we struck up a discussion about brown sauce and in which situations we used it over tomato sauce. The condiment-related conversation helped take my mind off things.

'Always on a roll and sausage, but never on a bacon roll,' I said.

'Me too,' said Stewart. 'What about macaroni cheese?'

'Broon sauce? No, tomato sauce.'

'Mince and tatties?'

'No, I don't put anything on my mince and tatties.'

'I put broon sauce on my mince and tatties.'

'I know – and it's weird.'

'Banana sandwich?'

'You've got to be kidding me.'

Mind you, this was the man who specialised in salad cream sandwiches.

In the meantime, we'd made it to the top of another hill.

Over the course of the next hour, I noted I was experiencing less pain less often. Whatever I was doing, it seemed to be working. I began to feel less afraid that all our plans might come to nothing.

I took another hill, applying a little more pressure on my right knee with no adverse effects. My knee accepted it and didn't bawl at me. That gave me even more confidence. Now I just needed to live with it and not do anything stupid. Break the rest of the day into bite-sized chunks. Take it easy, even if it meant covering the miles more slowly and us arriving far later at our destination.

My brother, at least, is a patient person. That was a good thing. He waited and encouraged me, being a good road-mate and a good brother.

This trip had become more of a challenge than I'd ever thought it would be. The truth was, I had no real handle on it. I was just in the middle of this thing, doing my best to cope.

As we descended a hill near Drymen, a group of boys on bikes cried 'Guten Morgen!' in unison. Did they think we were German? Were they German? Or were they having a laugh? With our white cycling jackets and black shorts, we could have passed for a couple of Germans, in that we were sporting the colours of the German football team.

'Are they – ?' I asked.

'Aye,' said my brother, answering my question before I'd asked it.

We got to pretty Drymen and threw our bikes down in the village square. For a blissful few moments, we lay on the grass, among the daisies and buttercups. I drank the rest of my water and went off to the shop to get some more.

When I came back, I noticed the two men sitting outside one of the pubs that face the square. They were having a pint and one of them was topless. In Glasgow at least, this state of undress, this condition, is known as 'taps aff'.

Taps aff is a weather-related status. When it's hot – by Scottish standards, which can just mean the sun being out – some men are wont to take off their tops and walk around bare-chested. You could be walking in Glasgow city centre and pass a bloke who'd decided it was a taps aff kind of day and to hell with it.

I'd never considered taps aff to be the best of looks. It also wasn't very practical. Surely the wearing of a cotton T-shirt would keep you cooler anyway? Never mind the potential damage you were doing to your skin.

The top half of a taps aff bloke can be anything from blinding white to worryingly red. It depends how committed the individual is to going taps aff.

The taps aff guy outside this pub in Drymen was at the in-between pink stage. Interestingly, his mate hadn't gone taps aff. In fact, he was as far removed from taps aff as you could be, seeing as he was dressed head to toe in leather biker gear. On a day like this too.

One guy overdressed, one guy underdressed. They made for an interesting pair.

Once taps aff bloke had finished his beer, he put his Celtic shirt back on. Then he put his biker jacket on over that, put on his helmet too, got on the back of his friend's bike and off they roared.

My brother and I departed Drymen with our tops on.

It took us some time to put some distance between ourselves and the village as we were immediately faced with a gradual hill climb that seemed to go on forever. As we climbed, the view unfolded and it was a cracker as we got a glimpse of Loch Lomond and an eyeful of Ben Lomond.

It was strange busting a gut with all this beauty around us. It was almost as if the surrounding scenery was a painting we weren't part of. We were somewhere else, divorced from this fine landscape, facing up to the physical challenge set by the terrain.

Even more bizarre, no sooner had we seen Ben Lomond to the west than we spotted Stirling Castle off to the east. If I wasn't mistaken, I could make out the Wallace Monument too. It was a beautiful clear day, but still. This really was confirmation Scotland is a small country. Not that it was making this bike trip any easier.

The hills came thick and fast as we climbed through an increasingly barren landscape. We reached the brow of our umpteenth hill and met a couple cycling south.

'It's downhill for you,' smiled the man.

'And it's downhill for you,' I was able to reply with some confidence.

After a glorious and seemingly endless episode of freewheeling, we rose again into the lovely hillside village of Gartmore, where we stopped for several minutes to get our breath back and admire the panorama south, which most definitely included the Wallace Monument.

From the pub across the road, we could hear the click of pool balls. Tempting though it was to sit in a pub and escape the rising temperature for a bit, we knew we needed to keep going. We hadn't earned another break yet. It hadn't been long since our last one in Balloch.

We kept going and a while later reached the town of Aberfoyle, where we stopped to load up on water and also picked up a couple of beers to enjoy later on. I had seen from the map that Loch Drunkie was coming up. It was too good a chance to miss – having a beer at Loch Drunkie. My brother wholeheartedly approved of the idea.

We would be earning it too by the time we got there because

there was a bloody big obstacle between us and Loch Drunkie – a gigantic climb through Achray Forest. I had heard about it from my curlew-baiting friend Alasdair, who had said it was tough and he was a proper cyclist, not like us pretenders.

Leaving Aberfoyle and taking to the forest track, it got very steep and difficult very quickly. There appeared to be no end to it either. How my knee was going to cope with this I wasn't at all sure. I dropped to the lowest gear available to me and stood up, trying to make some sort of progress. Eventually I came to a standstill and all I could do was get off the Green Lantern and push for a bit. I got back on and gave it another go, but couldn't sustain it. I soon came to a halt. The heat wasn't helping. The one good thing was my knee wasn't playing up. In fact, I had barely thought about it over the course of the past hour.

Meanwhile, Stewart kept climbing through the forest. I marvelled at his ability to do that. It was a tough climb and I wasn't too hard on myself. I had tried and failed, but it wasn't like the second day in Aberdeenshire where I'd been shown up for what I was: ill-prepared. This was different. A couple of hours ago, I'd thought I'd done myself a serious injury. I was grateful I'd got this far.

There were some strange sounds in the forest. I was struggling to identify them. It wasn't birds or any other kind of animal I could think off. Eventually I realised there was a zip slide in the forest and that somewhere nearby people were flying through the trees at a far greater rate than we were managing.

After an age, we came to the top, or rather Stewart came to the top and I got there sometime after him. I congratulated my brother on his efforts – he'd truly impressed me. Now it was time for the pay-off, the long descent that was all ours. I didn't deserve it as much as Stewart did, but I relished it all the same.

Hurtling down a forest trail is much more fun than hauling yourself up one. I didn't want it to end. It was enough to make me go 'whee'. It was very exhilarating, and the views were sublime. I figured the loch down below was Loch Drunkie – and sure enough, it was.

When we got there, we found a spot by the shore and cracked open our beers and savoured them in the late afternoon sun, grinning at each other, almost laughing. What a contrast to the grim morning. What a result.

Judging by the number of bottle caps lying around, others before us had also had the idea of a beer at Loch Drunkie. We'd take our bottle caps with us though. We weren't going to further spoil this idyllic spot in the Trossachs.

It was all downhill from Loch Drunkie, as we continued our descent at a rapid rate. So rapid in fact that my brother overshot the turn-off for Callander and I had to call him back.

The final part of the day's journey was a leisurely cycle along the southern shore of Loch Venachar, one of my favourite lochs. It was all down to the impression it made on me the first time I encountered it.

Clare and I were driving around the Trossachs on a gorgeous day when we passed this loch and thought we'd stop. We stepped down onto the shingle and saw the loch surface showing a perfect reflection of the opposite shore, the trees, the hills, the blue sky in a magical symmetry I've never forgotten. It was a perfect moment on a Sunday morning. I'd whipped out my camera and taken some pictures, but I really didn't need them. I was struck so much by what I saw that I've retained the image in my mind.

It was a slightly different day today and we were on the opposite shore, but it was still a delight to be reacquainted with the loch. I was so busy enjoying it that I didn't notice a bump in the path and almost did myself an injury. Had I been on a Chopper, I would definitely have come a cropper.

It wasn't long before we reached our shelter for the night, a Hansel and Gretel cottage just off the cycle path and by a river.

We checked into our cute B&B and helped ourselves to the complimentary coffee and shortbread in our room before freshening up and walking the 100 or so yards to the Lade Inn on the other side of the bridge.

The two of us ordered steak pie and chips and waded into some of the house ale. But after two pints, that was us. We were ready to pass out, or at least call it a night. A live band had just struck up in the room next door and the waitress told us they were 'the best around'. They were called Pure Malt and they sounded good, but we were pure knackered.

My brother and I left the pub to the sounds of 'The Braes of Killiecrankie'. We'd be going over those braes in the morning.

Back in our room and tucked up in our beds, with the calm rush of the river outside our window, I had a look at the route map to see what was in store for us come the morning, while my brother flicked through an encyclopedia he'd picked off the shelf.

'The circumference of the world is 24,896 miles,' said Stewart.

'Uh-huh,' I said, feeling my eyes closing.

'We're doing 1,000 miles on this bike trip.'

'So?'

'That means in two weeks we're doing one twenty-fifth of the world.'

'That's pretty impressive.'

'We could do the world in fifty weeks.'

'Sounds easy. Let's do it.'

Chapter 8

Loch Tay, go away

Day 8 – Callander to Aberfeldy

It was a busy table at breakfast as everyone filled their bellies for the day ahead. Among our fellow guests were Lance and Leslie from Australia. Well they had to be, hadn't they?

Lance and Leslie were on the trip of a lifetime. They were driving round Scotland and were just back from Skye. So far they'd loved it. In fact, the only thing that was bothering Lance was the sheer amount of summer daylight.

'Sunrise at 5 a.m., sunset at 11 p.m.,' he winced. 'Must be the adrenalin keeping me awake. I'll sleep when I get home.'

Also at the table were Craig and Marina, who'd driven up from York. Craig was from around here. He asked me and my brother where we were cycling to today. When I mentioned Balquhidder, Craig's eyes lit up as he described a three-mile walk from the village to a lochan that he and his best pal used to traipse to when they were kids.

'We'd go up there with our fishing rods,' smiled Craig. 'You drop down to it and it's there. It's the most beautiful spot, there's something about it. We'd fish all day and walk back.' He made it sound like paradise.

One time, he and Marina had come up and his pal had left out fishing rods for them so they could make their own trip together to the lochan. Listening to Craig talk about this special place made me want to see it for myself, but we'd no time for such sidetracking, pleasant though it would undoubtedly be.

I thought about my favourite place and the first thing that came to mind was the beach at Hopeman, specifically the east beach at the end of the beach huts, nearer to the Daisy Rock. We all have our places.

After one of the best bike ride breakfasts yet – I majored on the black pudding – we said cheerio to our fellow guests and pedalled into Callander to pick up some supplies.

On our way, we bumped into Hamish the Highland cow. Hamish was drawing in the tourists. A tour group was just getting off a bus now to check him out and have their pictures taken with him. The happy snappers were from the Far East and some of them wore Jimmy hats so as to blend in with the natives.

I knew another Hamish the Highland cow from a bedtime story that was currently one of my daughter's favourites. I read it to her often. This particular Hamish, however, was a mess. He had sweets tangled in his hair and his friends – one of them was a rabbit – thought it was high time Hamish had his hair cut. So they took him to the hairdressers. Of course, the hairdressers were sheep.

'Sounds like a good story, that,' said Stewart.

'I'll read it to you sometime,' I promised.

We left the real Hamish and landed on Callander's main street just as the shops were opening. One of them was a fancy bakery and lo and behold, did they not have genuine butteries! The Scottish croissant, the breakfast staple of my youth – even if we'd just had breakfast – on sale this far south. I never expected to find butteries south of Aberdeen, and even there they called them rowies. Stewart and I crammed a couple of butteries into our bags along with some tasty-looking sandwiches. We'd a long day ahead of us.

We left the bakery intending to set off, except that we got distracted by a toy shop. Seeing as it was open, we thought we'd check it out. Neither of us had been in a proper toy shop in years, and this looked like a *proper* toy shop.

We were stunned to walk in and end up straight back in our childhoods. These weren't any old toys. Many of them were favourite toys we'd had as kids. We gawped at glass cabinets full of old favourites. My first spot was General Lee, the car from *The Dukes of Hazzard*. Stewart pointed out James Bond's underwater car, which he used to play with a lot.

'Look!' said Stewart, now pointing at the Starsky and Hutch car. Then my eyes fell on my absolute favourite toy in the world, Thunderbird 2. I loved it so much I never let Stewart play with it, ever. The Thunderbird 2 in this shop was in mint condition. Most of the legs had long fallen off mine.

We moved on to a cabinet of tiny Corgi cars, several of which I recognised. I'd amassed quite a collection as a kid. My granda would take me to the Hopeman post office once a week and buy me one.

I used to take all my toy cars and line them up nose to tail in the lobby of our house on Dunbar Street. Dad, out of mischief, would move one of the cars slightly when I wasn't looking. I'd soon notice and have it back in its place.

I've noticed how my son likes to line up his toy cars. One day I moved one of them just to see. He was right on the case, putting it back in line and making everything exact. Like father like son, across three generations.

All my toy cars were in a basket in Mam's attic. As soon as we got back to Hopeman I was going to get them down so my son could play with them. Maybe he'd let me join in and we could make two perfect lines of cars.

Back in the magical toy shop, my brother and I moved through to the next room where we found more cabinets, these ones displaying dolls and action figures. I spied Tonto and the Lone Ranger, plus Ponch from *CHiPs*. This place was amazing.

There was even a red Chopper in the corner of the room. Goodness knows how I would have reacted had there been a silver Strika too. No doubt I'd have bought the damn thing, whatever the price.

I returned to the Green Lantern and Stewart to his White Knight and we left Callander, rejoining the cycle route north. The first few miles were on a flat and traffic-free path through woods. At one point we passed through a car park where a group of serious-looking cyclists were getting ready to ride. With their fancy bikes and snazzy gear, they looked like they knew what they were doing and I was reminded of my distinctly amateur status. It was great to see the cycle route busy though. There were lots of people out on their bikes, by far the most we'd encountered yet. We'd gone hours at a time over the past week without seeing any cyclists.

It was heartening to see so many children out with their parents. We passed three wee girls in quick succession, all being encouraged by their dads. The first girl still had her stabilisers on, while the next one was refusing to get back on her bike, despite her dad's best efforts to encourage her. The final girl was pedalling away with a huge beam on her face. 'Hi,' she said and we said hi back to the happiest girl in the world. Cycling behind her was the happiest dad in the world at that point in time.

We made our way along the western bank of Loch Lubnaig and on the edge of the village of Strathyre we stopped by a bend in the river to have our butteries.

'Do you think butteries are good for you?' asked Stewart.

'Oh aye,' I said, even though they're nothing but butter and salt. 'I reckon you could power your way round Scotland on butteries alone.'

'I'd like to see you give it a go.'

'I reckon I could do 10 miles to the buttery.'

'That's pretty impressive.'

'It's also a lot of butteries.'

After Strathyre, our next stop was Balquhidder. There were a few tourists visiting the grave of Rob Roy MacGregor in the kirkyard and we joined them.

'MacGregor Despite Them' read the inscription on the headstone. A few coins were scattered on the grave and there were a couple of whisky miniatures too.

It was a steady climb after Balquhidder and we reached a point where we could see right down Loch Earn. With a snaking river and trees in the foreground and the loch framed by the sides of the glen, it was the perfect picture.

Having taken a picture, we pushed on. Soon a group of children passed us on the path. They all had maps round their necks and looked to be doing a spot of orienteering. Moments later, we met a woman who asked if we had seen six kids. We most certainly had. She thanked us and went off after them.

Shortly afterwards we came to a section of the path that made our heads spin before we'd even tackled it. We were confronted with a sharp rise, the path zigzagging up to a significantly greater height. It's a good job it zigzagged, otherwise the path would have been vertical.

'Um,' said Stewart.

He'd said it all really.

A lot of leg and lung work was going to be required to get us to the top. I'd no doubt Stewart could do it. The big question mark hung over my head, but I was determined to answer it in a positive fashion.

I needed all the gears I had, plus a good dose of bloody-mindedness. Even when I was barely moving, I told myself I was going to make it. Turning all these sharp corners on such a steep hill made it doubly difficult. I swore a bit.

When I had almost joined my brother at the top, a group of walkers started coming down the hill. They strolled past in single file, every one of them smiling and saying hello like the cheery walkers they were. All I was able to offer in return, as I approached the summit of my personal Matterhorn, was a grimace. I hadn't the energy to say hello back to them.

When I got to the top, I stopped for the breather I'd been longing for. One of the last walkers in the group, an elderly man, put his hand on my shoulder and, smiling, said: 'Just think how good this is for you.'

I felt terrible.

'Thank goodness I've got all these gears,' I gasped back with an attempt at a crumpled smile.

Yet, in a way, it felt like the sweetest victory, especially on the back of all that anxiety over my knee the day before. So far today it felt fine. Long may that continue, I thought.

'Looking good,' said Stewart. I imagined I looked like death warmed up, but I understood what he meant and accepted his positive words.

We were soon in for a treat though, a spectacular ride along the Glen Ogle viaduct. Ogle means take a good look, so we did. This old railway line used to run to Oban. It would have been a remarkable train journey. It was a remarkable bike ride. Not that we were going anywhere near Oban.

We stopped for a minute to have a Mars bar and look back. How could it be that we could still see Loch Earn? I was rather annoyed by that. I thought we'd cycled much further.

After a long but gradual climb, we dropped through a forest with a fine view of a mountain in the distance. Before long we were in Killin, marking the midway point.

'We're halfway there!' I said.

Stewart thought I meant halfway to Aberfeldy but I meant in terms of the overall journey. It was lunchtime on the eighth day of our fifteen-day bike ride round Scotland.

'Fancy a half?' asked Stewart.

He'd read my mind.

We popped into the pub and took our beers out to sit on the stone bridge overlooking the Falls of Dochart. Adding to the spectacle were the motorbikes hopping and bumping on the rocks as part of some motorcycle trials. The riders all looked about twelve. They were being watched by proud dads.

These daring motorbike feats were reminding my brother and me of *Kick Start*, a telly show we used to always watch when we came home from school.

Though I've never ridden a motorbike I had a sudden memory of my most daring spell on my Grifter XL. One of my best friends, Graeme, had a Grifter too and we set up a stunt course in his back garden.

We made ramps using planks of wood and bricks. Then we tried to emulate Evel Knievel, had Evel Knievel ridden a Grifter. Graeme actually looked the part in his blue boiler suit. I don't remember either of us wearing helmets as we tried out our improbable stunt. Nobody wore helmets back then. The sheer recklessness of it all, it's amazing no one got hurt, besides collisions with bollards and landings in nettles. After a day of death-defying stunts in Graeme's back garden we dismantled the course and set it up at the park. I think our intention was to charge people to watch us, though I don't remember us charging anyone. I don't remember anyone watching us.

Some of the moves these young petrolheads were pulling off on the rocks in Killin were hard to believe.

'How did he manage that?' asked Stewart.

'Dunno,' I said, sipping my half-pint, 'but I reckon we've got the harder gig.'

Sitting at a table outside the pub was the group of road cyclists I had seen earlier in the day at the car park, the ones I'd taken for pros. They were all having pints and they were all smoking too. I had clearly overestimated them.

We left Killin and soon found ourselves cycling along the

southern shore of Loch Tay. Another group of cyclists passed us, coming the other way. 'Hi!' shouted one of them in an American accent. He sounded like the most enthusiastic man in the world. I decided I should be more like that. His was the kind of upbeat attitude I should be adopting for the rest of the journey. I needed to be more American and less Scottish. I was going to be like that man there.

'Go, go, go!' I called to Stewart by way of encouragement and he just ignored me. Well, that was the end of that. I accused my brother of being un-American and of cycling round the Scottish countryside in a Scottish manner.

'I'm Scottish,' he said.

This was true.

'Are we in Perthshire yet?' asked Stewart.

'Think so.'

Who knew where Perthshire was. Where did it begin and where did it end? Loch Tay sounded like Perthshire. Yes, we must be in Perthshire.

We were seeing Loch Tay in the best possible light too. The water was bright blue on the latest of our sunny days. Due to the presence and position of the sun, the hills on our side of the loch were actually casting shadows on the hills on the other side of the water.

Our appreciation of Loch Tay didn't last long though.

The road was hilly. They weren't big hills, but they were plentiful. Also, it was a narrow road. Every now and again there were passing places, but when we weren't near one we had to stop and pull in to the side of the road in order to let oncoming cars by. Of course, this always seemed to happen when we were on the middle of a downhill, forcing us to break and lose all the momentum we'd gained. We were unable to build up speed for the next hill, which was always just coming up. We never seemed to meet any cars when we were going uphill.

'Why is that?' I asked.

'Because they're waiting for us,' said Stewart.

The cars were timing it so that they could interrupt us on a downhill? You couldn't discount that possibility. Maybe they all had it in for us. The cars, the hills.

It was an up, down, 'after you' scenario as we pulled in for yet another car whose driver failed to acknowledge our considerate natures.

'They're acting as if we're invisible,' said Stewart. 'They could at least wave.'

'Arse,' I added.

Stewart then turned his anger on the road itself.

'There's no need for these hills. If they'd built this road 50 yards to the left.'

'Stewart, 50 yards to the left is in the water.'

'Forty yards then!'

There was no end in sight as far as Loch Tay was concerned. We were both getting thoroughly sick of the sight of it.

'I'm getting sick of this,' I said.

'Me too,' said Stewart. 'Is there an end to it?'

'Well, according to the map there is.'

'How far?'

'A wee while yet.'

I didn't tell him we'd barely cycled a third of the length of it.

We then got involved in a six-way stand-off between us, a car and three sheep. Confusion reigned. The sheep looked the most confused.

On our way again, we passed a sign: Welcome to Perth & Kinross, The Heart of Scotland.

We were glad to be here, if we could just get rid of this loch.

Later on we stopped – on another downhill – to let yet another car past. I stood my left leg on the grass verge, then realised I'd planted it in a bed of nettles. Not again.

'Ooh-ya,' I said.

'Stabbies?' said Stewart. Stabbies. I hadn't heard that word since I was a kid. Stabbies is what we used to call nettles.

Towards the end of Loch Long, I mean Loch Tay, we passed the Scottish Crannog Centre. 'Iron age life on the loch,' said the sign. I'd have quite liked to find out what iron age life on the loch was like, but they'd shut for the day.

'Gary, check this!' said Stewart.

My brother was pointing at a board advertising forthcoming local events.

'Festival of Nettles?!' I said.

'Festival of Nettles,' smiled Stewart.

'Good grief, we're not going to that.'

The festival attractions included nettle art, nettle spinning, nettle soap and nettle food tasting.

'Maybe they do a nice nettle and salad cream sandwich,' said Stewart.

A sandwich of bad bike moments.

When we reached the end of Loch Tay, we both let out a yell. We never thought we'd see the end of it and long before we did, we were sick of the sight of it.

It was teatime – though not yet our teatime – as we stopped for five minutes in the pretty village of Kenmore. White-harled buildings lined the square. One of them was a sixteenth-century inn reputed to be Scotland's oldest.

I could have murdered a pint, but didn't wish for the remaining miles to become murder, on the back of that long slog along Loch Tay. So we popped into the shop instead and got some more bananas and water.

Leaving the square, we cycled past a golf course. My brother told me that he and Dad had also played there once, in a competition. Stewart had played very well indeed and won a bottle of whisky. The organisers tried to take it off him and give him the prize of a golf brolly instead, since he was only sixteen.

'I'm not,' Dad had piped up, making sure the whisky went back to Hopeman.

It was only six miles now to Aberfeldy, but it was a tough six miles cycling into the wind. I felt my legs start to go again. I was finding that most days towards the end.

'It's always going to be that way,' said Stewart, who was feeling it too.

When you knew you were near the finish, your limbs didn't quite work the same anymore. Mental and physical tiredness took over.

We passed a sign for the village of Dull. I'd read about Dull in the papers. The people of Dull had been looking to twin with the city of Boring, Oregon. We considered dropping by to see how dull or otherwise it was, but we chose to forgo the diversion for the excitement of reaching the finish line.

Cycling through Aberfeldy, we found our way to our B&B for the night. Our host Cathy welcomed us and recommended a nearby curry house for dinner. It didn't disappoint. We cracked poppadoms, scoffed some pakora and tackled our curries.

We had plans for a couple of pints afterwards, but could only manage the one. It was probably for the best. We'd the Drumochter Pass to look forward to the next day.

I realised my knee had given me no pain whatsoever all day and was no longer concerned about completing the rest of the journey, so long as we stayed safe.

'I think I'm going to be fine,' I said.

'You're doing great,' said Stewart.

I just needed to stay sensible and finish this thing. My brother was doing brilliantly. He was flying and had not come near to suffering a characteristic mishap. Long may that continue, I thought. I'd received a text from our cousin Sarah which read: 'I thought Stewart would have fallen off his bike by now and been bandaged up like Mr Bump!' Yes indeed.

Before lights out in Aberfeldy, we watched a bit of telly in our beds. *The Lord of the Rings* was on and Frodo was halfway up Mount Doom, clinging to a rock and looking like he couldn't go on. Worse still, he'd run out of water.

'Take some of mine,' said his faithful friend Sam. 'There's a few drops left.'

Stewart laughed. 'That's like us.'

I supposed it was. The only difference was we weren't trying to save Middle Earth. We were just looking to get back to Hopeman in one piece.

Chapter 9

Drumming up the courage for Drumochter

Day 9 – Aberfeldy to Newtonmore

'I don't envy youse,' said Cathy, standing at her kitchen sink and filling up our water bottles. 'Maybe you should have a wee nip of whisky in them.'

Now there was an idea.

'Right,' said Cathy, handing back our bottles. 'Is that you? Raring to go?'

'Oh aye,' I said, doing my best to sound as if I was raring to go. Certainly we needed to go.

We thanked Cathy, who had given us one of the biggest breakfasts we had ever been faced with. Of course we stood up to the challenge, even if it was hard to stand up afterwards. But here we were, ready – if not raring – to go again.

Day nine on the road … my head hurt just thinking about it. I had woken up that morning and the reality of our situation had just hit me.

'Stewart,' I said, thinking he was awake.

'Uh-huh.'

'We've got seven more days of this.'

'Mm-hmm.'

'Seven more days – in a row. We have to get up every morning and do this, until THE END OF NEXT WEEK.'

'Aye, well, we both knew.'

We did, but I'd only just caught on. We faced seven more consecutive long days of cycling with no room for slacking off, no rest days. We had to get up each day, get on our bikes and cycle until we stopped. Such a routine made my head spin, even though I'd planned it. Eight days into our trip and it had finally sunk in. I found it mentally exhausting.

I tried not to panic as we set off on the latest instalment of this bikeathon.

It was a cool, cloudy day – perfect weather for cycling, except for the hint of a headwind. I hoped that we weren't going to have too much bother with that.

The cows were mooing, the crows were crowing and my brother was yawning. I too was yawning. I didn't have the energy for this, even though I really needed it.

The first few miles were spent working off our breakfasts. Cathy had cooked us an insane amount of food. We'd had the full works plus overtime. She had been overly generous with the portions and, by my reckoning, had toasted half a loaf of bread for us. I felt that my next meal would be breakfast the following day.

We got some early morning miles under our belt and glided through the village of Strathtay. I say glided – at least in my head we did. There was a great deal of activity going on in the village. The bunting was up and a marquee tent was being put up. Perhaps it was their gala day.

It reminded me of Hopeman at gala time. Each year Stewart and I were entered into the fancy dress competition. One year, Dad put me in a cardboard box. It was okay, the box had holes in it for my arms and legs to stick out and more holes for my eyes so I could see and another for my mouth so I could breathe. The box had been painted red and Dad had also painted a smiley face on the front of it. I was Mr Strong. The only downside was having to wear a pair of red tights to complete the look.

It couldn't have been a rainy day, otherwise my cardboard box costume would have been a disaster. Anyway, I came second. I can't remember who won, maybe Mr Tickle.

Another year in the fancy dress, Mam and Dad teamed up me and my brother as Popeye and Olive. Stewart got to be Popeye. I never thought that fair. I had to wear tights again – and lipstick. I think we came second.

At Logierait we crossed the River Tay on an old viaduct. After that, the road rose sharply, but it levelled out as we approached Pitlochry.

A fellow cyclist caught up with us and rode alongside us for a few minutes. He was doing a 70-mile circuit round Perthshire in preparation for a charity bike race from London to Paris.

'Two hundred and thirty miles in three days,' he said. 'Ferry from Portsmouth, finish at the Eiffel Tower, Eurostar back, hopefully the bike's there at St Pancras.'

We wished him all the best before he accelerated and left us for dust.

'Think I might look into doing a bike race sometime,' said Stewart.

'Really?'

'Aye, might as well.'

'Might not.'

Pitlochry, with its plentiful shops and cafés, was the perfect place for a pit stop. The main street was as busy as ever with tourists and we popped into a sandwich shop that appeared to sell a thousand different types of sandwich. I let my brother know my preference – pastrami and pickle – and left him to place the order while I went on a dual mission for coffees, plus two bottles of beer for us to enjoy later at the Drumochter Pass.

When I got back to the bikes with the coffees and beers, my brother looked to be in deep conversation with a man who was admiring his bike. It turned out the conversation wasn't that deep because the man, who was German, spoke very little English and my brother knew even less German.

'Good bike,' said the man, pointing at Stewart's bike.

'Aye,' my brother nodded. 'Do you cycle?'

'Yes, 4,000 kilometres.'

'4,000 kilometres?'

'Yes.'

'Cool.'

'Good bike.'

That was the end of the conversation.

We drank our coffees and left Pitlochry. It was 44 more miles to Newtonmore, where we were stopping for the night. Those 44 miles included the small matter of the Drumochter Pass, but we'd worry about that later.

Outside Pitlochry, we passed a campsite we'd stayed at on one of our family camping trips. When I think back to the summers of my childhood, we must have covered most of the country in a caravanette. I'm glad I got to see as much of Scotland as I did when I was a child.

If there was a soundtrack to those camping trips, it was *Brothers in Arms* by Dire Straits. I'd brought it along one time after buying the cassette version in Woolies in Elgin with some of my ice cream money.

Dad wasn't sure about Dire Straits. He wasn't into much music, besides Donovan and Dr Hook. But he let me put my new cassette in the deck and, by the end of the trip, Dad was hooked on Dire Straits. They'd become his favourite new band. I loved sitting up front with him, listening to 'The Walk of Life' as he drove us round the country.

Stewart and I continued north on our bikes, following the River Garry through the Pass of Killiecrankie. Approaching the Killiecrankie visitor centre, I requested a stop. I wanted to see the Soldier's Leap.

The Soldier's Leap concerns a dramatic tale associated with the Battle of Killiecrankie in which the Jacobites clashed with government forces. The soldiers were overcome by the clansmen in a short but bloody encounter in which thousands died. Some of the surviving soldiers fled south through the Pass of Killiecrankie, pursued by claymore-wielding clansmen.

During the terrifying flight, one soldier – Donald MacBean – was said to have made a mind-boggling escape. Chased by marauding Highlanders, he scrambled down to the rocky riverbank and made an 18-foot leap across the River Garry and lived to tell the tale.

My brother and I walked along the trail for a peek at the scene of this legendary leap. We looked down on a large flat rock at the frothy water's edge. From our perspective, it didn't look an impossible jump. Risky, yes. We were probably looking at it from a deceptive angle, plus we weren't being pursued by bloodthirsty warriors with muckle swords.

Getting back to our bikes, we bumped into our cousin Jonathan's girlfriend Claire, reminding us that Scotland is a small country. Claire was at Killiecrankie to perform a giant leap of her own. She was going bungee jumping for the first time. We wished her all the best. It seemed a very brave thing to do. I'd much rather cycle for fifteen days straight than take a jump from a great height, but then I'm no good with heights.

We made further inroads into the Highlands and pedalled through Blair Atholl, another place where the Sutherlands once parked their caravanette.

After Blair Atholl, we made a brief stop at the House of Bruar, the massive country emporium that sells everything from cashmere jumpers to smoked salmon. We didn't buy anything. We just used the bathroom and filled our water bottles from the sink. On the way back to our bikes, my brother bumped into one of his work colleagues, yet more proof that Scotland really is a teeny tiny place.

We'd reached the biggest part of the day – the point of no return. Not that we were thinking of cycling back the way. It was the point of no return in that there was nothing really between here and Dalwhinnie on the other side of the Drumochter Pass. We had our Pitlochry sandwiches in our bags and our bottles of beer. In hindsight, we weren't exactly carrying much in the way of supplies.

Setting off from the House of Bruar car park, we began the long, slow climb to Drumochter on a traffic-free road. After a while, we came to a sign.

WARNING
Drumochter Summit
Cycle track climbs to 457m
Weather conditions deteriorate without
warning and can be severe even in summer
No food or shelter for 30km

'Ach, we'll be fine,' I said.

'Nae bother,' said my bold brother.

Still, there was a sense of cycling into the unknown. We'd both done the Drumochter Pass plenty of times in a car going up and down the A9, but this was different, clearly.

'Do you think it'll be difficult?' asked Stewart.

'No idea,' I said.

As we made our way towards Drumochter, the climb did seem gradual, nothing too taxing apart from the fact that we knew it wasn't going to be ending anytime soon. The trees began to thin out and we were surrounded by hills and heather. There was a feeling of cycling at altitude as the hills got bigger and bigger and the weather turned a bit colder.

At times, we appeared to be cycling in the back of beyond. At others, we were right up next to the busy A9 on a grit path.

I didn't mind being close to the road, just as long as I wasn't on it. I much preferred it when we were away from the cars and lorries and it was just us and the sheep.

'We're definitely in the Highlands now,' said Stewart, as we passed a red triangle warning sign with a stag on it.

We seemed to be making reasonable progress. Off to our left, Loch Garry slowly revealed itself. I'd gawped at that view so many times from a car or train and did so again. It seemed a good spot to stop and have the sandwiches we'd been carrying since Pitlochry. My brother handed me my pastrami and pickle number. I bit into it and my mouth caught fire.

'Wow, that's hot,' I said.

'They'd run out of pickles, so I got jalapeños instead,' explained my brother.

'Cheers, Stewart.'

Now that the element of surprise was gone, the sandwich wasn't too hot to handle and I was able to tackle it in a manly manner. Fuelled by the jalapeños, I led from the front for a bit. It was growing colder and cloudier as we neared the Drumochter Summit.

When we got there, we took pictures of each other next to the big sign while the traffic rushed past. We then sat down in a handy roadside ditch, finding some shelter from the wind, and broke open the beers.

'Cheers,' I said, clinking bottles with my brother.

'To the rest of the trip,' said Stewart.

Following our al fresco brews, my brother decided he wanted to put on a pair of leggings for the descent. He was feeling the cold. I was feeling it too, but I didn't have a pair of leggings. I thought that I should probably get some.

Before he put on his leggings, Stewart first removed his shorts.

'I never thought I'd be standing at the Drumochter Summit in my drawers,' said my brother. If he'd been a little slower getting changed, it would have been embarrassing, because two women hill walkers appeared out of nowhere.

'We've been out since ten this morning,' said one of them. That meant they'd been in the hills for the past six hours.

'What was the weather like?' I asked.

'Fairly mixed. We were snowed on at one point.'

I asked if she wouldn't mind taking a picture of me and my brother with the Drumochter Summit sign behind us.

'Okay,' she said.

I handed her my phone and Stewart and I struck a pose, which we had to hold for quite some time as she was having some trouble taking the picture. I went over and showed her how it worked. It took her three goes and she kept saying sorry, but she got there in the end.

'Cheers,' I said.

'No problem,' said the woman. 'I hope it's okay.'

She walked off with her friend towards their car.

It was only after they'd gone that it occurred to me that they'd been out in harsh weather for six hours and the minute they'd stepped off the hills they'd been stopped by me asking for one of them to take a picture. No wonder she'd had trouble working my phone. Her fingers were no doubt numb and she'd walked away traumatised.

Still, at least we had our picture.

'Right, Mr Leggings,' I said. 'Let's go.'

'Ready when you are.'

Having been on a slow climb for the past hour or two, it was time to bomb down the hill to Dalwhinnie. That's what I'd been looking forward to, anyway. It didn't happen. We were hit by a strong north-easterly wind. Denied the fun of freewheeling, we were forced to pedal all the way. Life really isn't fair.

We arrived in Dalwhinnie much more exhausted than we should have been and discovered that there really wasn't much to Dalwhinnie besides a hotel and a filling station – and the hotel was closed. The sign 'Dalwhinnie, twinned with Las Vegas' just didn't ring true somehow.

We went over to the filling station and ended up drinking coffee in there with half a dozen other men who had been on a fishing trip.

'Catch anything?' I asked.

'Aye,' said one of them.

They weren't too conversational, so I didn't follow up by asking them what kind of fish they'd caught. I wasn't that interested anyway. Having drunk our coffees, we pushed on and battled with the wind some more.

The pretty village of Newtonmore was looking at its best as we approached it in the early evening sunshine. We soon tracked down the hostel and the owner asked how we'd got on. We told her that Drumochter hadn't been too tricky, but that the wind had been a nuisance.

'It's character-building,' she smiled.

Stewart and I had quick showers then went over the road to the Glen Hotel for dinner and a drink. According to the sign above the door, the hotel doubled as a Husband Day Care Centre.

> Need time to relax?
> Need time to yourself?
> Want to go shopping?
> Leave your husband with us!
> We'll look after him for you!
> You only pay for his drinks!

We ordered our meals and two pints of beer and I also asked for a packet of Scampi Fries.

'Old school,' said the barman, approving of the Scampi Fries.

Stewart and I went and sat down in the corner and my brother pointed out the saw hanging on the wall.

Above the saw it said 'Paul Daniels Stayed Here'.

'No way,' I said.

Had he sawn Debbie McGee in half in this very room for the entertainment of the good people of Newtonmore?

'Fancy a game of pool?' asked Stewart.

'Sure.'

He'd have been better off if he hadn't asked, because I was in red-hot form. I whipped him 3–0. My brother might be the sporty one of the two of us, but that night in Newtonmore he had no response to my wizardry with the cue. I was, after all, a former Hopeman café pool champion.

Stewart was better than me at football, golf and perhaps cycling too. But on the blue baize, I'd outsported him. I basked in the glory of my victory. I was allowed this small triumph. I spoke about my resounding win during our meal and brought it up again back at the hostel.

You have to seize on these moments of sporting success and go on and on about them.

Chapter 10

Fair Slochd

Day 10 – Newtonmore to Inverness

I jumped out of bed at 6 a.m., showered, got into my cycling gear, put some coffee on and filled up my water bottle. Keen to be on my bike, I think I was turning into a cyclist.

In my favourite book, *The Third Policeman* by Flann O'Brien, one of the policemen is – it's fair to say – obsessed with bicycles.

In this barmy but genius novel, the policeman in question puts forward the theory that when a man spends enough time on a bicycle, his molecules and those of the bicycle will interchange. This results in the man becoming part-bicycle and the bicycle part-man. Spend enough time on a bicycle and you could become, say, 90 per cent bicycle.

I reckoned that, at the age of seven, I was at least 86 per cent bicycle. Yet, until recently, there had been little trace of bicycle in me. Now, standing in the kitchen of this hostel in Newtonmore, I estimated that I was at least 73 per cent bicycle and that, in the coming days, that percentage would only rise.

Drinking my coffee, I thought about my friend Jonathan, who is a bike nut and once cycled the Pyrenees for fun. It was his idea of a holiday. My guess is that Jonathan is 98 per cent bicycle or thereabouts. Yet he still manages to function like a normal person. You can still go for a pint with him.

'What percentage of bicycle do you think you are right now?' I asked Stewart as he walked into the kitchen.

'Eh?'

It stood to reason that he was in the region of 73 like me.

'I put it to you that you're 73 per cent bicycle or thereabouts,' I said.

'Fine,' said Stewart. 'I'm 73. Can I have a coffee?'

'Sure, coming right up.'

It was a bit early for bicycle molecular theory.

We left Newtonmore with the sense that everyone else in the village was still asleep. They probably were. It was only 7 a.m. We'd never before set off this early. It felt good to be out and about at such an hour, as if we were stealing a march on the world.

Cycling through the gentle Strathspey countryside, we stopped at Ruthven Barracks near Kingussie. I'd seen these striking ruins on a mound countless times, going up and down the A9, but I'd never stopped to properly see them.

Ruthven Barracks was built on the site of an ancient castle by the government in order to tighten its grip on the Highlands, after the 1715 Jacobite Rising.

Following the Battle of Culloden in 1746, thousands of Jacobites gathered at the barracks with the intention of fighting on in support of Bonnie Prince Charlie. When the order was given to disperse – signalling the end of the rebellion – the defeated Jacobites set fire to the barracks.

What we were looking at now were the impressive remains. The castle that had once stood here was the power base of Alexander Stewart, the Wolf of Badenoch, who burnt down Elgin Cathedral.

We continued on our way and cycled past the wetlands of the Insh Marshes. It was an overcast day, but the only thing really troubling us was the northerly wind. We'd had it yesterday and here it was again. It made everything just that bit more difficult.

As we neared Aviemore, a succession of solo road cyclists raced past on their early morning runs. These fit individuals were indicating high percentages of bicycle in them, but they all said hello. Cyclists are polite sorts.

We saw a deer leaping through the trees and it seemed to be with us for ages. It would vanish out of sight, only to reappear again near the road.

The rain came on as we reached Aviemore. I was beginning to feel the cold and got off my bike to put on a pair of trousers. Cycling in them was hardly ideal, but it was all I had for my legs and I wanted to be warm. I had to get hold of a pair of leggings like Stewart.

Aviemore was a place we came to a lot as kids for short holidays. As a resort town, it had everything we needed. I remember going ice-skating and go-kart racing and playing the arcade machines. Best of all was Santa Claus Land, where it was Christmas every day of the year. You always got to meet Santa and you could visit the North Pole too. There were various rides as well.

The Aviemore of my childhood is long gone, the town having been redeveloped. But someone had told me recently that Santa Claus Land was still there, just boarded up. I decided, while we were here, we should try to find it.

'Stewart, we're going to Santa Claus Land,' I announced.

'Don't be daft,' laughed my brother. 'Santa Claus Land's long gone.'

'Well, I don't know. I heard it's still here.'

'Can't be.'

'Let's have a look for it anyway.'

Aviemore was fairly busy. It always is. I stopped a few people and asked them about Santa Claus Land, but got blank looks. Everyone I asked was a tourist. Eventually I got hold of a local who laughed and pointed down the road.

'It's all boarded up,' he said. 'You won't get in. There's nothing there.'

But I wasn't to be put off. We were in Aviemore and I wanted to go to Santa Claus Land.

We cycled down the road and came to a big blue boundary fence. In there was Santa Claus Land – and there was a gap in the fence.

'Are you sure you're meant to go in there?' asked Stewart as I climbed through the gap.

'Nope,' I said, emerging on the other side to find myself on what appeared to be a patch of wasteland. Although beyond some trees I could just make out the roof of a building.

Santa's Grotto!

I stumbled past broken branches and piles of rubble. The place was like a building site. I saw a chunk of wrought-iron fence decorated with a sad-looking blue spider and looked at the rusted remains of some colourful contraption on wheels. It wasn't Santa's sleigh because it had blades, not wheels. Scrambling down to the door of Santa's Grotto, I found it all boarded up.

Santa had long gone. I turned and got out of there as quickly as I could.

'Find anything?' asked Stewart.

'Just Santa's Grotto.'

'Was he in?'

'No.'

'Didn't think so. Let's get some lunch.'

We picked up a couple of pies from the baker's and my brother wanted a pair of gloves. Not to eat the pie with, but because his hands were cold. He went into an outdoor shop but came out gloveless.

'Twenty-two quid!' he said. 'For a pair of gloves? Might as well have cold fingers.'

I wondered when I was going to see about getting a pair of leggings.

Before leaving Aviemore, we dashed into a supermarket and

loaded up on water, bananas and Mars bars, this time adding Danish pastries to the mix.

Cycling through a modern housing estate and beneath a railway bridge, we wound our way along a woodland path, past pines and birch trees. The path ran parallel to a railway line and we were soon treated to the sight and sound of a steam train. Enjoying this off-road section of the route, we crossed a heather heathland with the mountains of the Cairngorms to the east.

Things were hotting up, weather-wise. I stopped to take off my trousers, half an hour after putting them on. I'd been too cold and now I was overheating. The variable Scottish climate was really slowing me down.

We reached the end of the off-road path, coming to a gate that had me stumped. I couldn't figure out how to open it.

'Here,' said Stewart, reaching forward to unlock it for me. 'You wouldn't be very good on *The Krypton Factor*.'

'When did they ever have to open gates on *The Krypton Factor*?'

Soon after we reached the village of Boat of Garten where we again heard the nearby whistle of the steam train.

'I once had an ice lolly here on a hot day,' I said to Stewart.

'Very nice,' he said.

It was only a few miles to Carrbridge and, according to the map, there were two ways of getting there. We could either take the B road or follow a farm track that would take us through woods. Stupidly, we picked the farm track. It was the more direct route judging by the map, but still the dumbest of choices.

Up we went on the biggest hill, dodging stones and boulders, and all the time I was thinking about the smooth stretch of road we might have been on. Halfway up the hill, I stopped. There was a fine view of the Cairngorms, dark mountains with traces of snow on their peaks and layers of cloud above.

But to hell with the view, this was a total waste of energy. We should have gone the other way.

'We should have gone the other way!' I said.

'Never mind that now,' said Stewart, 'We're here.'

I was spent and was all too mindful of the fact that we still had the Slochd Summit to tackle before the day was out, and that wasn't going to be a picnic. So why make life yet more difficult by adding this big headache of a supposed shortcut to our list of challenges?

'This is stupid,' I said. My brother didn't reply.

I was fizzing and starting to act like a child. It led to our first and only argument of the whole trip. We never argue, me and Stewart. This wasn't even so much an argument as me moaning and testing my brother's patience, of which he had a near infinite supply. It's rare for us to bicker and when we do, it's me.

'This is ridiculous,' I said, persisting with my well-worn theme.

'Go back then!' said Stewart who was beginning to get half-riled.

I thought I would go back. I'd go down that hill and join the B road, just for the hell of it. I would take the right road having taken the wrong one and make everything right again.

While I debated with myself, Stewart was carrying on. He'd had enough of me and was leaving me to my own devices to see what I wanted to do. He'd see me in Carrbridge. Of course, he knew fine well I was going to follow him and he didn't wish to waste any more time or energy arguing over the merits and drawbacks of the various routes to Carrbridge.

I stewed for a few more minutes, half got a grip of myself and got back on my bike to catch up with my brother who was now some distance ahead of me.

I made it to the top of the hill, but it brought no joy. I was still filled with regret. We should have gone the other way. What was wrong with me?

Even the descent failed to bring a smile to my face. As I pedalled along a stretch of woodland track, I scowled at a hare and gurned at a sparrow. How can you gurn at a sparrow? That's how bad I was. My mood was dark and my legs heavy as I caught up with my brother in Carrbridge.

'Well, that was a waste of time,' I said.

'Gary, we're here,' said Stewart, who, by now, would have been quite entitled to ditch me and finish the trip on his own.

We had stopped outside a pub that, according to a banner, had been voted the best in the region three years running. I peered in the window and saw a cosy scene with some inviting-looking ales on tap. What I most wanted was to go in, but I couldn't justify it.

We had the Slochd Summit to face. Dealing with that after a beer would only make it more of a struggle and I had no idea how much of a struggle the Slochd Summit was going to be. Certainly the wind wasn't helping us.

After an uncomfortable spell on a quiet road, though what traffic there was rattled along at a fair pace, we were relieved to land on a quieter path that would take us over the Slochd Summit.

I liked the word Slochd but didn't like the word summit. It sounded more suited to mountaineers than cyclists. Drumochter the day before hadn't been as bad as I'd feared, but how would this be?

A big black hill loomed in front of us. It looked terrifying. We were in the back of the back of beyond.

In the end, the Slochd proved tougher than Drumochter, but it didn't break us. Still, we were fair slochd by the time we made the top where a sign confirmed: Slochd Summit 1315ft (401m) above sea level.

We gave ourselves big pats on the back and proceeded on our way. We were also friends again after my meltdown between

Boat of Garten and Carrbridge. All it had taken was for me to wise up – and I finally had.

The sun was shining as we descended towards the village of Tomatin with the wind still working against us. We made a quick stop for a coffee then motored on towards Moy.

Moy meant one thing to me. A Hogmanay train journey from Glasgow to Elgin, travelling back to Hopeman for the bells and almost ending up taking in the New Year on the train.

It was well into the evening after a day of heavy snow when the train came to a halt some miles short of Inverness. After an eternity, it was announced that a tree had fallen on the line up ahead. Then came the uplifting update that 'a man from Moy is coming with a saw'.

I tried to picture this man from Moy, snow up to his knees, battling through the woods in blizzard conditions to reach this fallen tree that was preventing a train full of anxious passengers from getting home to their families for the New Year celebrations. After a tense wait, we received another announcement. The man from Moy had indeed cut through the tree with his saw, but another tree had fallen further up the line and the man from Moy was going to have to cut through that one too.

Everyone in my carriage started reaching into their bags and breaking open the booze. Had there been any musicians with instruments in the carriage, we would probably have ended up having a ceilidh. It was a real party atmosphere, with everyone making the best of a stressful situation. Then came the final update. The man from Moy had cut through the second tree and we'd soon be on our way. Everyone cheered. Thanks to the man from Moy and his saw, New Year had been rescued!

I thought about the hero of the hour now as we passed through Moy and wondered if he'd seen much emergency saw action recently.

With the blasted wind still in our faces, we caught our first glimpse of the mountains north of Inverness. We'd be meeting them tomorrow.

I then heard my brother say 'vroom' and figured that he'd lost it, pretending to be a motorbike. But he was saying 'broom'. We were surrounded by the bright yellow stuff and it was making me homesick.

'It smells like Hopeman golf course,' said Stewart.

It did too. We weren't that far from home, as this familiar, gentle landscape of green fields and yellow broom reminded us. But it would be days yet before we were back on Dunbar Street. We'd be seeing more of the far north first.

Then we caught our first sight of the Moray Firth since that second morning when we'd left Banff. What a welcome sight it was. Banff felt like a lifetime ago, even if it had been little over a week since we'd been there.

Just to top it off – this feeling of being almost home – we passed a farm and the farmer said 'aye, aye' to us. A very local greeting that. It's how folk in Hopeman say hello to each other.

The sun was really beginning to shine now.

'Always sunny in Moray,' said Stewart. We weren't quite in Moray, but close enough – and it did look like Moray.

I was enjoying seeing all these signs for Inverness. Mention of the Highland capital also made us feel like we were back on familiar territory, even though we'd be leaving Inverness in the morning for goodness knew what.

'Where are we cycling to tomorrow again?' asked Stewart.

'Ullapool.'

'And the day after that?'

'Durness.'

These were just words. What did trying to get to these places actually involve? Pedalling of course, but how big would those hills be (they looked big) and what the heck was the weather going to be like? At least we now had ten days of cycling under our belts. Surely that would count for something?

We cycled past the battlefield at Culloden where a few tourists wandered among the flags and then it was full pelt to Inverness. We raced through the eastern suburbs and arrived at our budget hotel close to the city centre. I fished my phone from my saddle bag and saw that I had a message from an old school friend, now Inverness-based.

'Are you in Inverness for the night or is it back to Hopeman for the chequered flag?' James was asking.

I got back to him and told him our plans. James, an avid cyclist, was keen to drop by our hotel in the morning and lead us out of Inverness and perhaps cycle with us for some miles. I liked this idea, and that was that.

My brother and I went out for a meal at a restaurant by the banks of the River Ness, then swung by the Castle Tavern for a pint in the beer garden, watching a glorious Inverness sunset.

The beer was a local brew from Cromarty called Happy Chappy and we were two happy chappies as we gazed at the pink sky and wondered what awaited us in the coming days. The north Highlands beckoned and, in spite of the unknown, I for one couldn't wait.

'Another pint?' asked Stewart.

'Aye, why not, eh?'

Chapter 11

To Ullapool and beyond!

Day 11 – Inverness to Ullapool

'Have you had your Weetabix?' asked James when we met him in the hotel car park after breakfast.

'Corn Flakes,' said Stewart.

'Bran Flakes for me,' I confirmed.

The two of us had opted out of the cooked breakfast and gone all cereal with a couple of croissants thrown in.

'Ullapool … you know it's up and down, don't you?' asked James, making hill motions with his hand.

My brother and I laughed. We were putting on brave faces.

'I'll take you the safest and quickest way out of Inverness,' said my old school friend who would be our guide and companion for the first part of the morning.

I asked James if he had a rope handy so he could tow us for the first 10 miles. It turned out he didn't, but he had everything else. Not only was James on a top of the range road bike, he was wearing actual cycling shoes.

'Aye,' he said. 'They take a bit of getting used to. First time I wore them, I stopped at traffic lights and forgot I was wearing them. Fell over.'

As comedy bike moments go, that must have been a good one.

But for James, cycling was a serious matter. Even his T-shirt told of a man who liked a challenge. It read: 'Iron Monster. 120K Loch Ness Solo Duathlon.' A demanding running and cycling gig – naturally, he'd completed it.

James had been fairly sporty at school, but not this sporty. He was well into his exercise these days and, as a fellow family man of a certain age, I admired him for this. At the same time, I wondered if I'd be able to keep up with him for the next hour or two.

My brother and I followed James through the streets of Inverness, amid the early morning traffic. It wasn't too bad. We just followed our leader. We stopped at a bike shop so I could pick up a pump to replace the one that had fallen off my bike somewhere in the hills south of Inverness yesterday.

I'd been looking forward to crossing the Kessock Bridge and it proved a treat in the bright morning sunshine. I took in the knockout views of the Moray Firth to the east and the Beauly Firth to the west, the water still and glass-like.

Looking east towards Hopeman, I told myself 'five more days'. Five more days and I'd be back on Dunbar Street with my family. We only had a few hundred miles to do between now and then. Two-thirds of our bike ride round Scotland was in the bag.

We reached the end of the Kessock Bridge and cut down a steep hill to cycle along a quiet road on the north shore of the Beauly Firth, as the gulls flapped overhead.

'Can three be a peloton?' asked James.

'Don't see why not,' I said.

'A pelican?' asked Stewart.

'Aye, a pelican,' I said. 'You're the beak and we're the wings.'

As we chugged along, James and I talked just a little about our school days. We had a class reunion coming up and wondered whether we would go or not. It was timed to coincide with us all turning forty. How did we get to this?

James and I spoke about our families and he told me the story of his fancy bike, how it had become a bargaining tool in the naming of one of his children. His wife had had her heart set on a name and James had been thinking about another name for his newborn.

'How much do you want the name?' he'd asked her.

She got the name, he got to splash out on a new bike.

James was busy putting together a bike trip that blew ours out of the water. He was intending to cycle and run from the Scottish Borders to John O'Groats, for charity as well as for the challenge. It was all very admirable. The difference between me and James was that my bike journey, if I was being honest, was probably a one-off. Whereas he pushed himself to the limit on a regular basis.

I resolved to be more like him, to do my best to keep this up once I was done. But I didn't sound very convincing to myself. I'd never do it. I'd return to my old ways and the bike would come out of the shed now and again when the weather was good.

Or maybe I could change the way I lived? I didn't live badly. It's just that there was no doubt it was good feeling this fit. I'd earned this sense of wellbeing over the past ten days and shouldn't just throw it all away.

In no time at all it seemed, we were saying cheerio to James in the village of Muir of Ord. He'd done more than a dozen miles with us and was going to cycle back to Inverness.

James wished us luck and off he went on his super-duper racing machine. He probably did the return journey a lot faster than the outward leg with us.

'He'd make Ullapool by lunchtime,' said Stewart.

I wondered when we'd get there. I hadn't the slightest idea, but get there we must. This wasn't a day for slacking off.

But it was a day that was really warming up. It looked like it was going to be another hot one. We'd been spoiled by good weather so far on this trip, though on a couple of occasions the sunshine had been more of a burden than a bonus.

We reached the tiny village of Contin where a sign outside a shop said it was the 'last shop before Ullapool'.

'Better stock up, eh?' said Stewart.

We wandered in to see what we could find.

Near Garve, we saw the Royal Scotsman train fly past on the line. Though that was fun to watch, the traffic flying past us on this A road – the only road to Ullapool – wasn't as enjoyable. We'd lorries, buses, cars and motorbikes to cope with and the two of us got a real fright when a taxi came close to clipping us. We shook our fists at the driver. Actually, we gave him the finger.

Every couple of miles, we'd stop in a layby for some respite. These frequent stops were slowing us down, but we often felt we needed a break from the chaos.

This was, for sure, the section of our route I liked least so far. We didn't have the National Cycle Network to fall back on any more. It didn't stretch to this part of the country and we wouldn't hook up with it again until Altnaharra in a couple of days' time on our way south again.

We were surrounded by stunning Highland scenery, but could see no further than the road. It required our complete focus. A sign said 'Ullapool 32 miles'. I was counting them down.

I once went to Ullapool as a teenager when I had a summer job with an Elgin cleaning company. This was after my ice cream days and wasn't nearly as much fun, but it was pocket money.

Me and my friend Andrew – who had taken a summer job with the same company – were sent up to Ullapool in a van. I can't even remember what the job was. I just remember sitting in the van feeling sick and dizzy with the strong smell of cleaning products and the frequent twists in the road. We occasionally came to an abrupt halt to avoid hitting sheep that had wandered onto the road.

Doing Ullapool on a bike was more fun than that, but only marginally so.

Just short of Loch Glascarnoch – a man-made reservoir with a massive dam – we were delighted to find a small café. I ordered a roll and sausage and Stewart settled for a pie. We added coffee to our healthy orders.

'Two hungry-looking faces here,' said the woman, bringing our food. 'Enjoy.'

We sat at the window, staring at the hills ahead of us.

'I take it the road goes through the hills and not over them?' said Stewart.

'I imagine so.'

A man came into the café and asked us where we'd come from and where we were heading. He told us we'd already done the hard part getting here from Inverness and that the remaining miles to Ullapool should be easier.

We were glad to hear this.

'All the best,' said the man as we left the comfort of the café for the discomfort of the A835.

When we got to Loch Glascarnoch, we stopped to chat to a man who was packing his fishing gear into his car. I asked him if there were much fish in the loch.

'Oh, you get everything in here,' he said. 'Mainly trout, Arctic charr, pike as well. Mind you, I've been up here four hours and didn't even catch my supper … another day!'

He asked where we were bound for.

'We're trying to get to Ullapool,' I told him.

'Bad weather supposed to be coming in,' said the man. 'But it'll maybe hold for a couple of days.'

'Let's hope so,' I said.

We got going again and were soon swallowed up by the hills. Boulders lay scattered everywhere, the hills looking like they'd been partially destroyed by some giant.

We passed a sign warning of strong crosswinds for the next mile. I swear that the minute we passed that sign we were hit by the crosswind which proceeded to batter us for the predicted mile before everything settled down again. It was weird.

The traffic continued to be a pain, one lorry getting a little too close for comfort. I thought we were going to get blown off the road. Then I noticed it was a lorry for that shortbread company I once worked for. I hadn't enjoyed it much then, and now they were trying to kill me.

We came to the Corrieshalloch Gorge and the Falls of Measach and decided to stop, stupidly thinking we'd be able to fill up our water bottles. Neither of us had paid much attention to the word 'gorge', meaning big deep thing with huge drop and the water well out of reach.

Still, we took a walk along the suspension bridge that spanned the gorge, just for the hell of it. Halfway across, I realised I wasn't so much thrilled as terrified. Prone to vertigo, I was now wondering why I'd so much as set foot on the bridge in the first place. I now wanted to go back, but my legs wouldn't let me. Rooted to the spot, I tried not to look down and then made the mistake of looking down.

'Stewart,' I said.

'It's fine Gary, it's safe.'

Just when I was able to lift a foot and think about walking back, we were joined on the bridge by a group of tourists, all of whom were behaving fine apart from one guy who thought he'd show off to his mates by BOUNCING UP AND DOWN ON THE BRIDGE.

'What the hell is he doing?' I asked my brother, as I gripped onto the bridge.

I glowered at the bouncing, grinning idiot but this made no impression on him. He was oblivious to my daggers, my look that wanted to kill him before he killed us all. We were on a suspension bridge. We didn't need added suspense.

'What is WRONG with you?' I wanted to shout.

And then he stopped. His mates hadn't been paying him the blindest bit of attention. My brother and I edged past them all and I resisted the temptation to kick Bouncing Man in the shins.

The steep drop of the gorge was reminding my brother of a family holiday in Spain when we'd all joined a donkey ride in the hills. Dad's donkey had seemed particularly hungry and kept wandering to the very edge of the track to nibble on what grass there was, giving Dad a good view of the drop that awaited him and the donkey, were the donkey to keep chewing until it had run out of grass.

I laughed at my brother recalling the donkey ride and then it hit me, the memory of a meal, the lunch we'd eaten that day at a farmhouse at the top of the hill, my first taste of paella. I could see and taste the prawns and smell the lemon. I saw us all sitting together happy in a shaded courtyard.

I hadn't thought about that day for a long, long time but I was right there now, with my family in the Spanish sunshine, even while Stewart and I were here in the heart of the Scottish Highlands.

As we edged nearer to Ullapool we faced a succession of hills. It also didn't help that, long before we got there, we were able to see Ullapool at the far end of Loch Broom. It wasn't so much a boost as a drawback, being able to see the place you're trying to get to long before you reach it. Ullapool was still miles away and remained a tiny target in the distance.

True to form, my legs started to pack in as we neared our destination. It was a similar story for Stewart. With the end in sight – even if it was a far-off sight – the mind was relaxing and the body was following suit.

Ullapool disappeared for a bit as we cycled with big hedges on both sides of the road, the hedges filled with blue flowers.

'Are they bluebells?' I called to Stewart.

'Think so,' he called back.

I spent the next half-mile wondering whether they were bluebells or not, which got me through the next half-mile. Then I didn't care anymore because I simply wanted to get to Ullapool, this town we'd been looking at for much of the past half-hour but never achieving.

Finally it happened. We turned up in Ullapool.

'Inverness to Ullapool … done!' I cried.

'We're getting quite good at this,' said Stewart.

Both of us were on top of the world. I really felt, right then, that we were capable of pretty much anything.

There were plenty of people out and about on the waterfront enjoying the sunshine and the view down the loch. Some folk sat outside having drinks and a few brave souls – students by the look and sound of them – were taking a dook in the water.

My brother and I went to check in at the bunkhouse I'd booked. Our spartan accommodation had bunk beds and just enough room for our bikes. We had everything we needed. The two of us ditched the bikes and went to the pub.

Standing at the bar, we got talking to a man who had driven up from Glasgow that morning.

'I'm knackered,' he said.

Now, hold on a minute, I thought. *We're* knackered. *We're* the ones who cycled here from Inverness – and left Glasgow on our bikes five days ago.

To be fair to the man, he went on to explain that, having driven up first thing this morning, he'd spent the afternoon working on a building site. This was him now winding down with the reward of his first pint of the evening.

We'd all done well to deserve this.

'Cheers,' I said and we all clinked glasses.

The man commented on how quiet the road had been, coming up. It was the viewpoint of a motorist. Being on bikes, we'd felt everything. It had been far too busy for our liking.

As Stewart and I left the pub to search for a chip shop, I clocked an old photograph on the wall. It was a cracker too, a black and white shot of the prizewinners in a pike-fishing competition. Men at the back with big moustaches and big fishing hats, boys at the front with beaming smiles. Laid out on the table in front of them all was a giant pike, likely the winning catch. But, best of all, dwarfing this monster fish was a pyramid of cans of McEwan's Export. There was whisky on the table too. It was a moment from the 1980s and as far as I was concerned it was one of the finest photos I'd ever set eyes on.

The chippy we found was doing a rare trade. As we waited on our suppers, a minibus pulled up across the street and out piled a bunch of mountain bikers.

'Look at them,' smiled Stewart.

They were walking with some difficulty, having to readjust to being back on two feet after a hard day on the bikes and being cooped up in a minibus.

Stewart and I scoffed our suppers by the shore in the warm evening air which was also full of menace. King rib supper and midges made for a frustrating combination.

I had a message on my phone. It was from James, back in Inverness.

'Were the hills as bad as thought? Enjoyed the catch-up this morning. 11 down 4 to go then!'

When put like that, it really did feel like we were on the home straight, albeit via the top of the mainland.

Before hunkering down in the bunkhouse, we dropped by another pub for a nightcap we probably didn't need.

We ordered our pints and sat at the bar as a man sat down next to us. It became clear he was a connoisseur of whisky as he told the barmaid he was a connoisseur of whisky. The man ran his eyes along the bar's extensive whisky offering, pointing out the ones he'd had (almost all of them) before settling on an Islay malt of a certain age that he thought he had not tried before.

He made a great play of ordering his dram, adding that he wanted plenty of ice. Once he'd been served this whisky he'd never experienced, he picked up the jug of water next to him and filled his glass to the brim.

My brother and I looked at each other.

As the man sniffed his glass and put it to his lips, there might just have been a trace of whisky in there.

Chapter 12

Donnie Darko moment

Day 12 – Ullapool to Durness

Given that we'd kipped in a bunkhouse and got up at the crack of dawn, our only option for breakfast was the local Co-op. And what do you know – they had butteries! Of which we picked up four, plus a bunch of bananas and a couple of cartons of orange juice.

'Breakfast of champions,' I said, as we stood on the pavement, chewing our butteries and washing our Scottish croissants down with the juice.

As we left Ullapool, a sign told us it was 173 miles to John O'Groats.

'To hell with that,' I said. We would be going nowhere near John O'Groats, but we still had almost 70 miles to cover to Durness before the day was done.

Immediately, we were hit by a big hill and straight after that an even bigger one. I issued my first swear word of the day and my brother joined me with some ripe cursing.

Looking back now, we'd little sense of what lay in store for us.

As soon as we'd struggled to the top of the second hill, we got a sudden gust of wind behind us, just when it didn't matter.

'Why didn't we get that five minutes ago?' moaned Stewart, taking issue with the wind's poor timing.

'Because it doesn't like us and is trying to do us in,' was the only explanation I could think of.

It was a cold morning and I'd on my new leggings, which I'd

picked up in Inverness. But my legs were half asleep. I needed them to wake up for this.

We came by a caravan site with a shop and popped in, mainly to get away from the cold. There was a pot of coffee behind the counter and I figured we could have some. I asked the man for two coffees.

'It's my son who takes to do with that,' he said. 'He's away on a wee job. He'll be back soon.'

I kind of wanted a coffee and so did my brother.

'What do we do?' I whispered.

'Maybe wait a minute,' Stewart whispered back.

I'd no idea when the man's son was coming back, but he did say soon.

'We'll give it five minutes,' I suggested to my brother and we had a wee wander round the shop.

After a minute or two, the man asked: 'Is it just coffees you want?'

Stewart and I turned and nodded.

The man reached behind him and poured two cups of coffee from the pot.

'That'll be £2.80,' he said.

We paid him and thanked him for our coffees.

'What was that all about?' asked my brother as we walked out the door.

'No idea,' I said. 'Drink your coffee.'

The coffees turned out to be the warm comfort ahead of the horror that awaited us, for the next hour was one of constant hill climbs.

'I hope it gets better than this,' said Stewart, blissfully un-aware, like me, that it was only going to get a lot worse. I counted twelve – twelve hills of pain, each more painful than the last. I was dying. My brother wasn't having a whale of a time either.

This was horrible. We were aware that we were in the north Highlands (i.e. the high Highlands), but this was a bit much, wasn't it?

By mid morning, the stuffing had been knocked out of me as the reality of the challenge hit me like a ton of bricks.

We weren't mucking about any more. Not that we had been, but – oh shit, here came another hill. Number 13, unlucky for us.

We struggled up it and got our first good look at Suilven, or at least some of it. Suilven is one of Scotland's most distinctive mountains, except we couldn't see the top of it, since it was mostly shrouded in cloud.

I turned my attention to the lochans as we passed two or three in quick succession. I got a surprise every time we came up a hill or round a bend and saw one. I didn't expect to see water at this height, but sure enough, here was another lochan, a big puddle in the sky.

My appreciation of the latest lochan was interrupted by a van driver trying to menace us off the road. We gave him the angry-Sutherland-on-a-bike gesture, the finger of disapproval.

Much more frightening was to come though. On the next long climb, we were both witnesses to the most bonkers manoeuvre, like an accident waiting to happen and a catastrophic one at that.

The scenario was this: A fuel tanker crawling up the hill and being overtaken by two cars. That in itself was madness, but they made it, thank heavens. The problem was the third car behind them. The driver had hesitated, unsure whether to go or not. Just when it looked like they might hang tight and wait for a clearer opportunity – say, on the other side of the hill – they decided to give it a go.

My brother and I looked on in horror. They had no idea what was coming. We hoped it was nothing. We consciously slowed down, so as not to be too near any of this: fuel tanker, overtaking car, hill, possibly other cars coming in the other direction.

The two of us breathed huge sighs of relief when we saw the car nip in front of the tanker before the top of the hill and not kill anyone. What an idiotic thing to do. It had been a complete gamble, endangering the lives of how many? There might have been kids in that car. I felt sick.

A driver, racked by indecision and seeing other drivers in front take the chance, felt the pressure to overtake a fuel tanker on a hill and finally went for it. What about anyone else? Why take the risk? I couldn't get my head round it.

After miles of nothing but hills, lochans and reckless motorists, we saw a sign for a tearoom two miles ahead.

'Stewart, a tearoom!' I shouted for the first time in my life.

Two more miles and we would be sitting down having a cup of tea, or more probably coffee, and maybe a biscuit or something, living the dream.

We pedalled like the clappers, stopping just the once to take pictures of each other next to the massive 'Welcome to the county of SUTHERLAND' sign. We even put on our best Sutherland faces. The Sutherlands in Sutherland ... we were going to be in Sutherland for some time.

Tearing down the final stretch, we reached the tearoom and it was shut.

'It's shut,' said Stewart.

'Why's it shut?' I asked.

'Flippin' hell,' said Stewart.

'Arse,' I chipped in.

It was the only thing we'd been looking forward to, a tearoom in the middle of nowhere. What was a tearoom in the middle of nowhere doing being shut on a Wednesday morning?

This was the trouble with this part of the country, for us at any rate. You could go for many miles without finding anything and even when you did find something there were no guarantees.

We consoled ourselves by delving into our bags and bringing out our back-up butteries from that morning find in Ullapool. We ate them quietly by the roadside and moved on.

Grimly grasping our bike grips and scowling in the face of a northerly wind, we made our 523rd hill climb of the day. I felt like I'd bagged several Munros.

'See on our next trip?' asked Stewart.

'Aye.'

'Can we not just drive across America in a Cadillac?'

'Where would the fun be in that?'

'You call this fun?'

The hilarity continued as we tangled with the hills and wind until we caught a break and freewheeled down to the wonderfully named Inchnadamph, where we stuck our heads into the hotel but there didn't seem to be anyone about.

The closest thing to any sign of life was the fish on the walls, stuffed and framed catches of hotel guests down the years. We checked some of them out on our way back from the bathroom, having filled our water bottles at the sink.

'Caught in West Assynt, Mr Thomson, July 1908, weight 5lbs.'

That, by the way, wasn't Mr Thomson that was caught. Mr Thomson caught a five-pound fish.

'Caught in Mid Assynt, Mr Clay, June 1895, weight 9lbs.'

'Caught on Loch Gruagach, W H Valentine, June 1927, weight 6lbs.'

And so on.

I noted the set of scales by the door on the way out. I liked the idea of being a guest at the hotel and returning from a long day's fishing to slap down some trout in order to weigh up the success of my day.

Just after the hotel, we passed an old kirk, where a sign read:

OPEN
THURSDAYS
1.30PM–4PM

'Och, we've missed it,' said Stewart.

But we did manage to stop at Ardvreck Castle. Its ruins over-look Loch Assynt and we read – on an information board – something of the history of the castle which was the seat of the MacLeods of Assynt and the scene of numerous sieges.

'Look, Stewart,' I said, pointing at the board. 'Says here it's haunted.'

'All castles are haunted,' said my brother.

But I read on in any case.

The castle's resident ghosts included the weeping daughter of a MacLeod chief. She had drowned in Loch Assynt sometime after marrying the Devil in a pact to save her father's castle, and her ghost was often seen by the loch.

Then there was the tall man in grey, most often seen among the ruins. He was an altogether happier ghost, apparently. What did he do? Dance? Juggle?

I scanned the loch and the ruins in the hope of seeing a ghost out of the corner of my eye. But all I could see was the group of German motorbikers in leathers who had also decided to stop and check out the castle.

After Ardvreck – a good name for an aardvark too, I think – we faced the 646th hill climb of the day. Halfway up, I stopped to hold on to one of the snowpoles at the side of the road. They came in pretty handy. Looking back to where we'd come from, I saw a bird of prey swoop down on Loch Assynt for its lunch.

A couple of hills later, I announced: 'There's a downhill coming!'

'Heard it before,' said Stewart, destroying my optimism.

Sure enough, what I'd thought was the top of the hill was just the road levelling out before rising again.

'Good God,' I gasped.

But a mile or two on, joy of joys, we were treated to the best section of the entire trip so far. We'd climbed as high as we could go and – for now – the only way was down. What a down it was too. We looked ahead and saw the road wind down for what seemed like miles before it snuck behind a hill.

'Enjoy it while it lasts,' I said.

'Oh, I will,' said Stewart.

I went first, then my brother overtook me and I just let him go. Maintaining my own steady speed, I just watched him race off ahead of me. My eyes were fixed on my wee brother, flying free amid this majestic landscape. It was one of the finest sights I'd ever seen. It was all worth it for this.

Eventually we came to the tiny village of Kylesku and cycled down to the hotel on the shore which overlooked Loch Glendhu and Loch Glencoul. You would be hard placed to find a hotel in a prettier spot. A fish van had just drawn up with a delivery.

We went in with the idea of having lunch. The place was busy, but we found a table by the door. I quite fancied a half pint of the local ale, but the morning had been so tough and there was so much yet to come that I was frightened off the idea and had a soft drink instead. My brother did likewise and ordered a BLT and chips for his meal. Seeing as we were in a waterside restaurant that seemed to specialise in seafood, I opted for the crab.

I hadn't realised that the crab would come whole and that I'd have to tackle it myself. I'd never tackled a crab before. I'd been given what appeared to be a pair of pliers. I gave it my best shot and set to work on my crab. Stewart watched with amusement while he munched on his BLT.

'Bugger,' I said, putting down the pliers after another failed attempt. This was the most frustrating meal ever. I didn't need this right now. I needed a burger or something. Or, if it really had to be seafood, fish and chips. Why had I ordered a crab?

'Why did you order a crab?' laughed Stewart.

'No idea,' I said.

I picked up the pliers again and managed to crack open a bit of the crab and find what looked like a piece of crab meat.

'Are you supposed to eat that bit?' asked Stewart.

'I'm not sure.'

I ate it anyway. It was nice, but there wasn't nearly enough of it. So I ordered a bowl of chips.

While I was waiting on my chips, I picked up a copy of the local newspaper and read that one local community was being connected to the Ullapool water supply via a new pipeline. I also discovered that there had been national recognition for the outstanding beauty of the area's beaches.

'Thought for the Week' was provided by Jack Kerouac: 'Live, travel, adventure, bless, and don't be sorry.'

Kerouac wasn't from around these parts, but I kept that thought.

After a wholly unsatisfying lunch – it was entirely my own fault – we got back on the bikes and continued with the theme of hills, stopping at the top of one to take in the panorama from a viewpoint with a useful board that spelled out everything we saw, including Gaelic names and meanings.

Loch a' Ghlinne Dhuibh … loch of the black glen …

Loch Gleann Cuil … loch of the glen at the back …

Those were the lochs the hotel overlooked when I'd been too busy wrestling with my crab.

Loch a Chairn Bhian … loch of the white cairn …

Beinn Aird da Loch … mountain of the high point between the lochs …

A Ghlas Bheinn … the grey mountain …

None of these names would look out of place on a map of Middle Earth. Back on Planet Earth, matters were getting worse the further north we went.

To compound the never-ending hills and the growing head-wind, we were now having to cope with the dreaded midges too. This was the worst combination. We stopped to apply some anti-midge spray, whatever good that would do.

I once went to a wedding on Skye and, during the course of the evening, stepped outside the hotel in my kilt for some fresh air. Within seconds my knees had been bitten to bits. These mainland midges didn't seem to be as ravenous as the Skye version, but they were still a pain.

We passed the ominously named Badcall Bay and came to the village of Scourie, where we wandered inside another hotel whose walls were covered in fish.

We particularly admired a near nine-pound whopper of a brown trout caught on Loch na Thull as recently as 11 May 2005. Fishing rods and nets were also on display, as well as glass cases full of fishing flies with names such as Silver Doctor, Black Spinner, Orange Fly, Jock Scott, Durham Ranger and Dusty Miller.

'They sound like drugs,' said Stewart.

'Either that or porn star names.'

We noticed that some guests in the lounge were being served tea and scones. We asked about this at reception and were told to take a seat. Sitting in our deep armchairs near the fireplace, we scoffed scones and drank coffee.

'Can we just stay here the night?' asked Stewart.

It was a thought. We were still something like 25 miles from Durness and the afternoon was wearing on.

At the other end of the lounge, an elderly gentleman rose from his armchair and revealed his true height. The man was a spindly giant. He creaked slowly past us.

'Treebeard,' whispered Stewart. He did have the look of an Ent.

We settled the bill for our coffees and scones and the woman at reception asked where we were cycling to.

'Durness,' I said. It sounded so far away just saying it.

'Well, it's not too bad,' she smiled, instantly lifting my spirits. 'The roads are a bit winding.'

I noted that she hadn't said hilly.

Before we properly set off we stopped at a shop to see what we could find to sustain us for the remaining miles. My brother picked up a bunch of bananas and took them to the till.

'How much?' I heard him ask.

They turned out to be pretty expensive bananas, but he bought them anyway. We needed them.

'Bananas must count as an exotic fruit up here,' said Stewart.

'Bananas are an exotic fruit,' I said. 'They don't grow in Inverness.'

'How far have we got to go?'

'A sign back there said 25 miles.'

'How far back?'

'About a mile?'

'Hmm.'

'Better get going,' I said in a tone more suited to 'better get to bed'.

The first hill after Scourie wasn't too taxing.

'I think it's getting easier,' I said.

We then turned a corner and got hit by a blast of northerly wind.

'I'll just shut up then,' I suggested.

We then had to struggle up a hill that, according to a sign, had a 12 per cent gradient, which sounded steep and it was. It actually felt more like 90 per cent, but that would have had us falling down the hill and not making the marginal progress that we were making.

My brother suggested the idea of a 12 per cent beer called Gradient. 'Renders you legless', was his suggested tagline.

The hill after that wasn't so much 12 per cent as 12 miles long, or so it seemed. It was as tough as any we'd encountered, particularly with the wind against us. But the beauty of this particular hill climb – if there was any beauty in it – was the presence of little mounds of sand by the roadside. You could pedal for a bit and stop to plant your left foot on one of the mounds of sand and have a breather – then set off for the next mound of sand a little further up the hill and stop there too.

These mounds of sand helped break up the climb. They were like stepping stones to the top. Sometimes you would go to put your foot on one of them and find a footprint already there – it wasn't my brother's either as he was behind me. These were footprints of other cyclists who had been through the same thing we were going through now, forcing our way up this damned hill. It made us feel less alone (though we were very alone).

At tiny Rhiconich, we came to a police station.

'Should we hand ourselves in?' I asked.

I took out the map – a page ripped from an old road atlas since we didn't have a cycle route map for this part of the country. I wanted to see where Rhiconich was in relation to Durness. The map made for more pleasant reading than the last time I'd looked at it. We weren't out of the woods – or rather the hills – yet, but the map was beginning to reassure me and not scare me.

The sky was a worry though. Over the sea to the west, it was clear blue. But ahead of us to the north, where we were bound, it was growing steadily and more worryingly black.

'That doesn't look good,' said Stewart.

'No.'

We then saw our second bird of prey, swirling in the sky and getting ready to swoop.

'What is it?' asked Stewart.

'A bird of prey,' I said.

'Aye, but what kind?'

'Dunno, an eagle.'

'Doesn't look like an eagle.'

'Something else then.'

Not being able to identify a bird of prey was the least of our problems.

We cycled towards the angry-looking clouds as the landscape around us became ever more weird and wonderful to the point of being frightening. The hills were strewn with random boulders and rocks. With very little else to look at, I kept looking at them. It began to get unnerving.

Sometimes it would be one big boulder sat on the top of a hill. Then a few together would form a shape. One big boulder with two smaller rocks behind it resembled a giant rabbit's head. It was all going a bit *Donnie Darko*.

'Stewart, can you see the rabbit?' I asked.

'I can see the rocks.'

I tried not to stare at the stone rabbit, but it was looking back at me. It really was freaking me out.

I then managed to scare myself further with the sudden thought that we might not make it. We really were nowhere. We could become stranded here and no one but the giant stone rabbit would know – and he wasn't going to tell anyone.

I needed to pull myself together. I tried talking to my brother.

'You know these mountains are millions of years old?' I said.

'Really?' said Stewart. 'I thought they'd just been put up yesterday.'

Some comfort he was. Though he did offer some encouraging words a while later when we passed a sign telling us that Durness was 14 miles away.

'That's Hopeman to Elgin and back,' said Stewart.

And when he put it like that …

Mind you, we had no idea what those 14 miles were going to be like.

'Smaller mountains,' said Stewart, showing more positivity. The hills did seem to have calmed down a little bit.

I kept my head down, got a grip of myself and tried to swallow up those last 14 miles as fast as I could, with the wind still fighting us.

As afternoon became evening, we caught our first sight of the Kyle of Durness. The tide was out, leaving large swathes of golden sand. The last few miles cycling alongside this vast stretch of sea and sand seemed to take forever, the wind in our faces and not letting up for a second.

A car went by – the first one we'd seen in a long time – and the driver gave us the thumbs up. That gesture alone raised our spirits.

The nearer we got to Durness, the stronger the wind got. Thank goodness we were cycling on a reasonably flat road because I was just about done in. About a mile short of Durness, an approaching car pulled up.

'Gary?' said the driver, leaning out of the window.

It was Tony, the owner of the B&B we were staying at. We were well past my estimated time of arrival. Tony and his wife were heading to the local school with their daughter for parents' evening. He said they wouldn't be long, but that there were other guests back at the house so we'd be okay for getting in.

'There's some home-made banana cake on the table, so help yourselves,' said Tony. 'See you in a bit.'

As we rode that last mile at the end of an epic day that had kicked off twelve hours ago in Ullapool, all I could think of was that banana cake on the table. It had become the thing I wanted most in life – that and a hot bath.

'Welcome to DURNESS (Diuranais)' said the sign as we entered the village. 'Please drive carefully.'

It might as well have said 'Please collapse carefully in a heap'.

I don't know how, but we'd made it.

When we got to the B&B, we met our second Australian couple of the trip, who were touring the whole of the UK in their car. The husband asked where we were cycling to. My brother and I were both struggling to speak, but between the two of us we were able to give him an idea of the trip.

'Is it fun?' asked his wife.

'Eh,' I said, not really knowing the answer to that.

'Not so much today,' said Stewart.

She then asked if we'd seen the Aussie flag her husband had draped over the Welcome to the Highlands sign.

'Which one?' I asked, trying to focus after one of the hardest days of my life.

'The Aussie flag,' she replied.

'No,' I said. 'Which sign?'

'The Welcome to the Highlands sign.'

I couldn't ask again, so just said I hadn't seen it. This conversation was giving me a headache. Either that or the twelve hours I'd spent tackling mountains and a northerly wind had scrambled my brain. They seemed a nice couple, but I wasn't fit for any of this.

Just then a new guest arrived, another cyclist. He was soaked to the skin, having been caught in a downpour that must have occurred within the past ten minutes – lucky us.

The man had cycled all the way up from Altnaharra. We were heading that way in the morning. Boy, what a thought. Not only had he biked up from Altnaharra, he'd stopped off along the way to climb a Munro.

'You what?' asked Stewart.

'Yes, I went up Ben Hope,' said the man.

'Then got back on your bike and cycled here?' I asked.

'Yes,' he said, taking off his dripping wet cagoule.

'Was it fun?' asked the Australian woman.

Chapter 13

Baked tatties and Russian dolls

Day 13 – Durness to Lairg

It was fortunate that we were able to join George, the mountain-climbing cyclist, for breakfast because he shaved 10 miles off our journey from Durness to Lairg.

My brother and I had been intending to cycle along the north coast as far as Tongue and then head south for Lairg. But George pointed out that we could turn south much earlier at Hope on a single-track road that ran down the side of Loch Hope. This was the road he had come up yesterday, when he'd stopped to climb Ben Hope.

'It's a lovely cycle too,' said George.

We thanked him for putting us on the right track and asked where he was heading after breakfast. George was aiming for Cape Wrath, after which he was coming back to Durness and carrying on to Tongue. He was doing all of this today, though he wasn't looking forward to the predicted easterly wind set to be in his face all the way from Cape Wrath to Tongue.

I reckoned he should just forget about Cape Wrath and head straight for Tongue, but I didn't say that. Just as I was a man with a plan, George had his plan. It might be tough, but it would be done.

'You're not climbing any mountains today, are you?' Stewart asked him.

George shook his head: 'No, not today.'

Easy-peasy then.

After a bumper breakfast, Stewart and I forced ourselves up

from the table, wished George the best of luck and went to pack our things. 'Did you see George with his breakfast?' asked Stewart, folding his clothes into his backpack.

'How do you mean?'

'He must have chewed each mouthful twenty-three times.'

'I didn't really notice.'

'Twenty-three times at least – amazing.'

'Well, he can't take that much time with his cycling, not with the sorts of distances he's covering.'

'He stops and climbs mountains!'

'Oh aye, so he does. Yes, he's some man, George.'

I wanted to be more like him – apart from the mountain thing.

'Where's Lairg?' asked my brother.

'That's where we're heading.'

'I know, but where is it?'

'On the way home.'

'That's handy.'

Before we set off, Tony, our host, offered to drive us to the shop so we could get some supplies for the day ahead. We wouldn't be passing too many shops between Durness and Lairg. On the way back from the shop, I asked Tony about Durness's John Lennon connection.

'It's that one over there,' said Tony, pointing out the house that had once been owned by Lennon's auntie. The future Beatle had many happy childhood holidays here on the north coast. Durness has made something of its John Lennon link too. After we said goodbye to Tony, the first place we went on our bikes was the John Lennon Memorial Garden, a small landscaped affair beside the road. Several stones in the garden had inscriptions. One read:

> There are places
> I remember all my life

Having done the John Lennon Memorial Garden, we then paid a visit to Durness's other big tourist attraction: Smoo Cave. For some reason, the word 'smoo' put me in mind of the Moomins.

Smoo Cave turned out to be a bloody big cave.

'Check the size of it,' said Stewart once we'd climbed down the steps to the cave entrance, which is the largest of any sea cave in Britain. We felt quite tiny standing there.

The cave has two chambers, the first shaped by the sea and the inner one formed by a river. I wanted to check out the inner chamber with its waterfall.

'You coming?' I asked Stewart.

'No,' said my brother, shaking his head. He was staying put.

There are some colourful tales attached to Smoo Cave. One concerns the henchman of powerful clan chiefs, who was said to have murdered a number of people and disposed of their bodies by chucking them down the waterfall into the cave. Another tale involves a man who sent his dog into the cave to see if the Devil was there. As the terrified dog scampered back out, the Devil, in a rage, blasted his way through the cave roof, creating the blow hole that exists today.

Of course, that's all bollocks.

'You sure you're not coming in?' I called to my brother from the inner chamber.

'Yes,' I heard him call back.

The waterfall effect was pretty cool, but I was beginning to get a little freaked out hanging about on my own in a cave. It wasn't helping us get to Lairg either, so I decided to come out.

'How was it?' asked Stewart.

'Dark,' I said. 'And watery.'

We left Durness and followed the twisting road along the north coast, getting occasional views of golden beaches. It wasn't long before we reached the massive sea loch that is Loch Eriboll.

The map seemed to show that we had to cycle two-thirds of the way round it in order to continue our journey east.

At least it gave us some dramatic scenery to look at. Who was I kidding? We'd been fed dramatic scenery for days now. I'd had it up to my ears. After a while, you became fairly blasé about it. Ah yes, another mountain. Oh look, a sea loch.

The road down the west side of the loch wasn't too hilly, but it was narrow. That there were frequent passing places was just as well. We'd a few campervans to look out for. They were okay though. The drivers were mostly taking their time on a road that was no doubt unfamiliar to them. Not remotely in a hurry, they were playing it safe.

The same could not be said for the local tradesmen, racing to their first jobs of the day. They didn't hang about. They knew this road like the back of their hands and were something of a hazard to us as they careered round corners.

Heavy grey clouds clung to the hilltops. I was looking out for something – besides rogue tradesmen – as we looped around the shore of Loch Eriboll. And I spotted it too, near the top of a hill that rose above the loch.

'Look,' I said, pointing.

'What?' said Stewart.

'On the hill.'

'Clouds.'

'No, not the clouds, the stones.'

'It's not another stone rabbit, is it?'

With the low clouds, the visibility wasn't great. Nonetheless, I could just make out the pattern of stones laid out near the top of the hill. I'd been looking out for them as I'd read about them while researching our trip.

Loch Eriboll was a popular Royal Navy anchorage during the 1920s and 1930s. All those decades ago, crew members scrambled up this hill and spelled out the names of their ships with stones that still remained. It was hard to make out the names of the ships from this angle and in this weather – and I wasn't about to crawl up the hill to find out. But I was pleased to have spotted them.

'Hey,' I said to Stewart. 'We could spell out the name of Dad's boat.'

'What, *Adonis*? But he was probably never here in his boat.'

'No, but we're here.'

'On you go then.'

But instead of climbing a hill and carefully laying out a pattern of stones – it's maybe more something that mountain-climbing cyclist George would have done – we pedalled on with a mild breeze in our faces.

Eventually we reached the bottom of the loch, or rather the southern end of it. Our bikes were good, but they weren't submersible. We sat down for five minutes and admired the lochan across the road from the loch. Its surface showed the perfect reflection of a nearby hill.

Back on the bikes, another campervan was coming our way. The driver was smiling and mimicking us, doing a pedalling motion with his hands when his hands really should have been on the steering wheel. Mercifully, he didn't keep this up for too long and didn't veer off the road and into Loch Eriboll because he'd been too busy riding an imaginary bike. We gave him a wave anyway.

The next car we encountered slowed down and the driver leaned out of his window to say to us: 'Watch oot for the beasts!'

My brother and I hesitated. What beasts?

'From the hills!' laughed the man. 'The ones with the horns!'

We were getting nearer to the truth.

'The Highland cattle! They're all on the road! Good luck!'

And with that, he was off.

We continued on our merry way and, rounding a bend, saw a

swarm of orange in the distance, the very ginger gang of High-land cows the man had spoken off, taking up the road.

'I hope they'll let us through,' said Stewart.

'Are they dangerous?' I asked.

'Don't think so.'

'What about the horns?'

We approached the hairy crew with some trepidation.

I have a real fear of cows. It's ever since that time I did the coastal walk from Hopeman to Lossiemouth and, passing a field, saw a cow turn round and run at me. I started running too. I wasn't taking that fence for granted. This belligerent beast might crash through it or try to leap over it and land on my head. My peaceful walk had been shattered by a cow that, for whatever reason, was trying to kill me or at least knock me into the sea. I kept running until I was well past the field, and didn't look back.

'There's no way that cow was trying to get you,' said Stewart.

'Why was it chasing me then?'

A cow had tried to hunt me down. From then on, I'd decided they were capable of anything.

'What are we going to do?' I asked as we stopped to ponder the Highland cow roadblock.

'We could try shooing them out the way,' suggested my brother.

'How do you shoo a dozen Highland cows?'

While we were discussing tactics, a car appeared on the scene, coming in our direction. We watched as the cows shuffled aside to let the car past. Once it was through, the cows closed ranks again.

'Bugger,' I said.

I considered asking the driver of the car to give us a lift back through the cows. But what about our bikes? In any case, he'd just passed us. He didn't even wish us luck. It was okay for him in his metal car.

These cows weren't going to shift for us and I wasn't even going to give them the opportunity.

'How about we cut down onto the shore and get round them that way?' I suggested.

'Eh?' said Stewart. 'That looks a pain in the neck.'

'Well, I can think of a worse pain in the neck.'

'All right. Let's give it a go.'

'It's our only hope,' I said, sounding like Princess Leia in *Star Wars*.

We left the road and clambered along the rocky shore with our bikes until we were well past the cows and could return to the road with no further bovine intervention.

I took a picture of my brother on his bike with the Highland cattle on the road behind him. We had succeeded. We had overcome the cows.

Soon after that, we turned our backs on Loch Eriboll, winding our way up a steep hill before making a rapid descent and crossing a bridge over the River Hope. We were then confronted by a hill with a 15 per cent gradient.

'I think this is the worst one yet,' said Stewart as we battled up it, working those gears to full effect.

'Bloody hell,' I gasped as a van cruised down the hill and the driver shouted: 'Keep going!'

Mercifully, we didn't have to keep going right to the top as we reached the turn-off for the road that would take us down the side of Loch Hope, as recommended by George at breakfast.

At last, we were heading south for real and Hopeman felt that little bit closer. Here we were too, a couple of Hopeman men cycling alongside Loch Hope.

Loch Hope rang a bell, actually. What was it? Oh yes, it was around here that my pal Alasdair was attacked by a curlew.

'We'd better be on our guard,' I said to Stewart, reminding him of my friend's traumatic encounter with a furious, big-beaked bird.

'What was it again?' asked Stewart.

'A curlew.'

'Might have been a pterodactyl.'

'Don't think pterodactyls are native to the Highlands, Stewart. They're more common to Perthshire.'

'Is that not panthers?'

'Aye, them too.'

I scanned the sky above Loch Hope for any sign of a feathered foe. But flying menaces with random grudges against cyclists were the least of our worries, because soon enough we came up against another cow roadblock.

'Aw, not again,' I said.

'Don't worry,' said Stewart. 'There's only three of them this time.'

'That's still three too many.'

There was no way round this trio of Highland cows. They took up the road and that's all we had to work with.

We faced Daddy Cow, Mummy Cow and Baby Cow. Baby Cow was cute, but Daddy Cow was a real worry. He was huge with massive horns. What to do? The three just stared at us. They weren't going anywhere.

'I'll go first,' I said.

'Eh?' said my brother, rightly surprised.

'Seriously, I'll go first. Just follow me.'

I'd decided to grab the bull by the horns, so to speak. I wasn't going to lie down to a bunch of cows, plus we had to get past them sometime today. It wasn't like me to be so bold, but I just wanted it over with. And I wanted to conquer my ridiculous fear of cows.

I pedalled as slowly as I could towards them, keeping my head down and not looking them in the eye. Mummy Cow shuffled to the side a bit and that gave me some space. I was careful not to go too near Baby Cow as I didn't wish to upset its parents. As I passed Daddy Cow, he gave me a low grunt. I'd made it through the cow roadblock, my brother right behind me.

To be honest, I don't think they'd been that bothered by our presence. We were more concerned about them. They were a pretty docile bunch really. I'd always thought that about Highland cows, but had never really wanted to find out for myself. Relieved to have dealt with this uniquely Highland obstacle, we pressed on, hoping that we wouldn't have to negotiate any more of these beasts.

Apart from the cows, the path was good and the everchanging views of the loch and the mountains were outstanding. We even found the perfect picnic spot – a grassy patch by the side of the road – and stopped for some lunch. Looking out over the loch, I don't think I'd ever eaten in a better spot. The clouds were clearing too, revealing patches of blue sky.

I got stuck into a vegetable samosa I'd picked up in the shop in Durness, while Stewart tackled a steak slice. We shared a side salad of crisps. For pudding, we had more of the banana bread from the B&B. It tasted as delicious as it had done on our arrival the night before.

I checked the time. It was just after noon. In little more than 48 hours we'd be on the final stretch to Hopeman. We'd come a long way since that beautiful Sunday morning on Dunbar Street almost two weeks ago and we'd soon enough be at the back gate again.

After climbing back on our bikes we cycled in the shadow of Ben Hope, which dominates the southern end of the loch. Ben Hope is Scotland's most northerly Munro. We couldn't get a proper sense of the scale of the mountain as much of it was shrouded in cloud, which only made this dark mass of rock look even more foreboding.

'I can't believe George got off his bike and went up there yesterday,' I said, peering up.

'Aye,' said Stewart. 'He's some man.'

We passed a sign saying: 'Way up'. Next to the sign lay tangerine peels, telling of climbers who had set off from here. Maybe they were George's tangerine peels.

When we reached the bottom end of Loch Hope, we emerged into another wide glen with a grassy plain. As it revealed itself, it struck me that it was one of the most wonderful sights I'd ever seen. Stewart loved it too. It was these rare moments that made all the pain worth it. I felt lucky to be standing here with my brother.

One side of the glen looked diamond encrusted, the scree sparkling in the sun. It was impossibly beautiful and the unexpectedness of it all added to the charm of this special place which we had all to ourselves as we'd made the effort to get here on two wheels.

The wind tried to push us back as we cycled down the glen. It was funny how the wind had completely switched direction since yesterday, to remain in our faces. But it didn't seem to bother us as much. I felt content, as happy as I had been in a long while.

We came to the remains of a Pictish broch. Dun Dornaigil had been built thousands of years ago and held a commanding position in the glen, which was probably why it had been built here, perched on a natural terrace overlooking the plain. We parked our bikes against the broch and had a wee walk round it. Then we were on our way again.

Soon we started to climb eastwards onto a plateau. Wherever I looked, I was knocked out by the views, with mountains in every direction. This was as remote as I'd ever been, at least since yesterday. We'd likely never be here again and I did my best to savour the experience. It took my mind off the cycling, which in itself wasn't too bad. The sense of isolation was different from yesterday's. This time I felt more confident about our progress. These hills weren't scaring me so much.

I looked back over the past fortnight. It felt a long time since the dolphin centre at Spey Bay and the end of an exhausting second day when we'd collapsed on the grass outside King's College in Aberdeen. Going for a dook in Stonehaven seemed like ages ago, as did the Southside Shuffle in Montrose.

After miles of nothing but hills and heather, we stumbled across a lochan. Then, with the wind properly pummelling us (it had switched direction again, it seemed), we began our descent towards Altnaharra.

We didn't stop when we got to Altnaharra, even though it was the first settlement of any note we'd seen in a while. The two of us kept pedalling amid the rolling moorland until we came by a pub in the middle of nowhere.

It was the Crask Inn – the hanging sign squeaked in the wind – and we were going in. We parked our bikes against the wall and entered a lobby where a woman wearing tartan trews emerged to greet us.

'How are you getting on?' she asked.

'Oh, we're fine,' I said. 'Just on our way to Lairg.'

'The wind's not been with us,' said Stewart.

'When it is,' said the woman, 'you feel like an athlete!'

She had that right.

'If it's coffee you're after,' she said, 'come through here. If it's beer you're wanting, the bar's through there and my husband will see to you.'

We knew where we were going. My goodness, we'd earned this.

We entered the bar. There were a few tables and chairs – there was no one in but us – as well as a fireplace and a dartboard. I tried to picture this place when it was busy and imagined it was a great crack. I'd fallen in love with the Crask Inn and we hadn't even been served yet.

I wandered over to the window.

'Stewart, look,' I said, pointing at the array of items on the window sill.

'Pack of cards ... marbles ... Jenga ... Russian dolls ... baked potato.'

It was true. There was a baked potato on the window sill. I tried to think of a game involving a baked potato, but couldn't come up with one. Also, it wasn't an unbaked baked potato. It had been baked, not eaten and put on the window sill.

'Maybe it's a lucky baked potato,' said Stewart.

'Could be.'

Just then a man appeared behind the bar – the woman's husband – and asked what we were after. We were after two beers and he recommended some from the Black Isle brewery. He'd just put it on. We were heading to the Black Isle tomorrow, so thought we might as well get a taste for it now.

We were swithering over whether to have our usual half pints or stretch to a full pint. We still had some miles to go.

'Where are you heading?' asked our landlord.

'Lairg,' I said.

'In that case, you should have a pint.'

We went with his judgment.

'It's downhill all the way to Lairg,' he said, as he poured our pints. 'You'll be there in half an hour.'

Having served our drinks, he had a wee taste of the beer himself, chatted for a bit, then disappeared.

My brother and I were in awe of him. He'd replaced George in our eyes.

We were halfway through our nice pints when his wife appeared.

'Ah, my favourite knife!' she said, reaching for a giant blade I hadn't noticed on the counter. Off she went with it, to chop up whatever it was.

We didn't see either of our hosts after that. Having finished our pints, we got back on our bikes and bade farewell to the Crask Inn. It had been a complete one-off, but I hoped it would be repeated. I intended to come back one day, whether by bicycle or some other mode of transport.

It wasn't quite downhill all the way to Lairg. We were hit with an initial climb, just after that pint as well. My legs were beginning to come undone, just as they always did at this time of day, but I managed up the hill in the blazing sunshine. In the past half-hour, the weather had turned glorious. We'd been so lucky with it for the majority of this trip.

After that, it was the promised long descent as described by the landlord at the Crask Inn. Stewart and I hunkered down torpedo-style and tried to gain as much velocity as we could with the least amount of pedalling. It was a fun way to end the day, one last blast before Lairg.

I couldn't believe it when we passed a sign saying it was only two miles to Lairg. We'd covered the 10 or so miles from the Crask Inn ridiculously quickly. Our man had not been far off with his half-hour estimation.

'That was fast!' said Stewart as we whizzed into the village and were greeted by the sign:

Failte An Luirg
Welcome to Lairg
Crossroads of the North

Looking back on another long day in the saddle, it had been against wind much of the way, but that stop and pint at the Crask Inn had helped power us over the line.

We arrived at our B&B where we met our host Win, who

kindly offered us coffee and shortbread. We sat down for a chat and very soon another guest turned up on a bike. David was a retired clergyman from England and was cycling much further than us over a longer period of time, while raising money for a church in Baghdad where a friend of his worked.

We asked David about his journey and he described to us and Win a few of his experiences so far. 'You can't help but talk about it,' he smiled.

We asked where he was heading next. Orkney and Shetland were on the cards, as were the Outer Hebrides and St Kilda. I wasn't aware that you could do St Kilda on a bike and was surprised he was even contemplating it. Phew. And I'd thought George was the intrepid traveller.

After our showers, Stewart and I went to the pub across the road for a meal and a game of pool. I went easy on my brother this time. We got chatting to the barman and told him we'd stopped at the Crask Inn earlier.

'Ah, the Crask,' he smiled. 'I wet my baby's head at the Crask Inn.'

He then told of his night of celebration at becoming a dad, a slap-up meal and drinks with friends. It sounded good to me.

Chapter 14

Fortrose: The Final Frontier

Day 14 – Lairg to Rosemarkie

The weather the following morning was dreadful. It was enough to make you hide indoors, except we couldn't.

We joined David for breakfast. He was hoping to catch a train to Thurso in half an hour, but was worried they might not have room for him as the trains only took a limited number of bikes. And there weren't many trains to Thurso. If he wasn't allowed on the train, he faced an 80-mile cycle in foul weather.

After David left the breakfast table, I said to Stewart and Win, who was making more coffee, 'I hope he makes it.'

'We'll never know,' said Win. 'My life is full of unfinished stories.'

How true that must be, I thought. People came, people went. We were passing through on our own adventure.

My brother and I polished off our breakfasts and got ready for our penultimate day in the saddle. We thanked Win and hit the road and the puddles. It really was the dreichest of days, but we'd been lucky so far. Most days had given us sunshine. If anything, it had felt too hot to cycle at times, which was pretty remarkable for Scotland, even in the months of May and June. Though the wind had been cruel to us on occasion. One thing I had learned over the past fortnight was that the wind can be more of an enemy than the hills.

There was only the faintest of breezes this morning, but we were going to get soaked. The clouds were heavy, the rain relentless. As we cycled on a very nice but very wet road through woodlands, a Scottish Water van flew past. Then my brother got splashed with some Scottish water when I cycled at speed through a puddle and he got sprayed in the face.

'Thanks for that,' he spluttered.

After a few miles in weather more suited to species with gills, we reached the Falls of Shin. The Falls of Shin sound like some sort of bike accident, but they're actually a popular tourist attraction. People flock to see the spectacle of the falls and the salmon leaping upstream to their spawning grounds.

A group of tourists was just getting off a coach now as we got to the car park. They all stood in the rain, waiting for their guide to hand out the brollies, by which time they were already soaked.

My brother and I wandered into the visitor centre, dripping a fair amount of excess rainwater onto the floor. We were met by Mohamed Al-Fayed, or rather an unsettling wax figure of the Harrods owner in full Highland regalia. The Falls of Shin lie within his Highland estate.

I asked one of the staff in the visitor centre if there was any chance of us seeing the salmon, not knowing whether it was a good time of year or not.

'If they want to leap, they will,' said the woman. 'July, August and September are the best months.'

It was June. We weren't going to see any leaping salmon. Not that it mattered. We'd seen dolphins leaping, so leaping salmon weren't such a big deal. We took a wander down by the falls anyway. Unsurprisingly, given the weather conditions, they were gushing. But really, we were standing in the rain looking at water.

'Think we should go,' said Stewart.

'I was thinking that myself.'

We left the Falls of Shin and continued our journey south. A lorry loaded with logs rattled past, giving us barely any room.

That was way too close. I gave the lorry driver the fingers, but I doubt he saw me. Judging by his driving, he wouldn't have cared.

Our surroundings were beginning to change and look more like home again. The moors and heather had been replaced by green fields and yellow broom.

'No mountains either,' said Stewart.

'Yep, no mountains,' I agreed. We were done with them, thank goodness.

But this rain just wouldn't let up and when we reached the village of Edderton we sought cover in a bus shelter. While we lingered, we read some of the Tippexed graffiti. Someone had scrawled 'Beetlejuice' on the bus shelter. 'JR' was there too. This was an '80s bus shelter. 'Metallica' were also present. Wherever there's graffiti, there's always Metallica.

We left the bus shelter to get soaked again and just before Tain had to negotiate an unexpected and scarily busy roundabout. Shaken by the experience and the cold, we dropped into Glenmorangie Distillery to chill out and warm up.

We weren't after a drop of whisky or anything. We just wandered round some of the whisky-related exhibits in the visitor centre for ten minutes. I learned that the necks of the distillery stills were as tall as an adult male giraffe. I was now picturing a drunken giraffe stotting about.

There was a display on whisky and the movies which featured pictures of various film stars enjoying a dram. But it was the old newspaper cutting that really caught my eye.

'Whisky And Ooo-La-La!' was the headline.

And the sub-heading: 'Brigitte orders thirty-six cases.'

I read on.

'Guess who's the latest convert to Scotch whisky? None other than that blonde bombshell, the original sex kitten – Brigitte Bardot.'

The French actress had been staying at a hotel in East Lothian while shooting a film in Scotland. The manager of the hotel's 'renowned 999 cocktail bar' – a fairly alarming name that for a cocktail bar – had done such a good job of selling whisky to Brigitte that she'd had some of it shipped back to France.

The bar manager told the paper: 'Brigitte and the crew have developed a taste for straight malt whisky. The only time they ask for champagne is for celebrating after a successful day's filming.'

So either they were downing whisky after a disastrous day's filming or they were knocking it back first thing in the morning.

We left the distillery and cycled into Tain where we popped into a café and ordered soup and sandwiches for lunch. The man at the next table asked us where we were going. We told him we were bound for the Black Isle. He said he had three kids who were all into their bikes and that we were making him think he should get back into cycling himself.

'Haven't had a bike in years,' he said.

'Go for it,' I said.

'Might look into it.'

'Just don't try to cycle from Ullapool to Durness,' Stewart warned him.

'Was that a tough one, then?' the man laughed.

We both nodded.

'Enjoy your lunch,' said the man, rising from the table. 'Shame about the weather.'

It was a shame. We were still thawing out. But we felt much better when the waitress brought over two giant bowls of tattie and leek soup and two substantial tuna sandwiches.

It's a funny thing, soup. I've so many strong memories of bowls of soup I've eaten, whether it be Dad's fish soup or tattie soup at my granny's or that bowl of oxtail soup I had while my Strika was being stolen. Or did I just remember that oxtail soup because of the trauma of the bike theft?

We polished off our tattie and leek soup in Tain and made easy work of our sandwiches. That was us sorted for the rest of the afternoon. While we'd been tucking in, the rain had stopped too. Everything was taking a turn for the better.

Our next target after Tain was Tarbat Ness. It wasn't quite on the way to Rosemarkie, where we were stopping for our final night on the road. Tarbat Ness involved a bit of a detour, but I was determined for us to get there.

There's a lighthouse at Tarbat Ness, which is across the Moray Firth from Hopeman. Every night you can see its light shining from the village. One certainty of growing up in Hopeman is seeing the lighthouse at Tarbat Ness. I wanted us to go there and gaze back across the Moray Firth to Hopeman. And maybe wave. Not that anyone would see us, but I liked the idea of experiencing the reverse view of the one I'd grown up with. Plus it wasn't too much of a detour. The good thing was Stewart was up for it too and didn't need any convincing. It was adding a few miles to our day, but it was just something worth doing.

We headed towards Tarbat Ness on a long stretch of straight road. It was windy, windy, windy. It had really picked up and we were being buffeted about, but we both had the bit between our teeth and were doing our utmost to power along and devour those miles.

The wind aside, this was about the most comfortable I had ever felt on a bicycle. It was partly the big increase in fitness over the past two weeks, but it was the adrenalin too. I was excited about reaching Tarbat Ness. I could only imagine what it would feel like tomorrow, closing in on Hopeman.

We pedalled through the fishing village of Portmahomack, which put us within a mile or two of the lighthouse. Then we cycled down an avenue of yellow broom with seagulls flying overhead. We were approaching the tip of the peninsula and I could see the red and white striped stick of rock that was the lighthouse, rising in front of us. It looked good enough to eat, but you'd break your teeth biting into a lighthouse.

As soon as we got there we sat down in the grass to the sound of the sea breaking on the rocks and seagulls crying. We looked out over the Moray Firth, but there was fat chance of seeing Hopeman on a day like this. We could hardly see 100 yards into the water because of the fog. I waved anyway. We'd be seeing Hopeman tomorrow.

Having made it to Tarbat Ness, we now had to get to Nigg to catch the ferry to Cromarty. We were talking a dozen miles, but what were a dozen miles to us? We'd become invincible, sort of.

We passed through Portmahomack again and a schoolboy with a satchel on his back called out to us: 'Like your bikes!'

'Cheers!' we shouted back. Any appreciation of the Green Lantern and White Knight was appreciated.

The dozen miles to Nigg turned out to be the fastest dozen miles of the trip. We flew like the wind with the wind backing us for a change. Our timing was perfect too as the next ferry was just about to depart. A ferry worker yelled 'Come on!' and waved us forward. We hesitantly pedalled down the slipway and onto the boat. The tiny ferry only takes a couple of cars, but there weren't any. It was just us. We paid the five pounds each for our passage to Cromarty.

Our voyage on the *Cromarty Queen* across a choppy and foggy firth only took about fifteen minutes. At the other end, we pedalled off the boat and up a slipway over seaweed, while avoiding a couple of rocks.

A young boy was doing pretty impressive wheelies on his bike at the pier. It's a picturesque place, Cromarty, with its pretty whitewashed houses, but we couldn't afford to hang about. The day was wearing on and we still had to get to Rosemarkie. At least we had set our tyres on the Black Isle now.

Stewart joked about still having his sea legs and not his bike legs as we climbed the hill out of Cromarty. The fog was really closing in now and was giving us cause for concern. All the cars had their fog lights on and we didn't have any lights. Visibility was worsening by the minute and neither of us felt comfortable on this road. It was the quickest route to Rosemarkie but it also felt dangerous.

I checked the map and saw there was a turn-off coming up that would take us on a longer and more winding route to the place we were trying to get to. It was actually the designated route on the cycle network. It meant more miles, but surely less traffic and that was all we could wish for.

We got off the main road and entered a dreamlike world that had us enveloped in the fog. We were surrounded by fields with hay bales and crows. Strangely we could feel a sea breeze too, but then the map had us cycling close to the coast, even if we couldn't see it.

After a few miles, with the fog clearing a little, we caught one of those joyous descents that seem to last forever. We free-wheeled for such a long time that I never thought it was going to end and neither did I want it to.

Finally, we rolled to a stop and were forced to pedal for a bit until we came to a junction. We turned right and only real-ised we were going the wrong way when we saw a bus marked 'Rosemarkie' going in the other direction. Easy done.

We turned round and just as we were descending into Rosemarkie we saw a cyclist coming up the hill. When he got closer, I suddenly realised who it was.

'James?'

'Aye, aye,' said my old school pal.

I tell you, Scotland's a small place.

It also seemed such a long time ago that he'd led us out of Inverness and accompanied us on those early miles towards Ullapool, but it had only been a few days earlier. To think of all that we'd seen and accomplished since then. It was good to see James now.

'How you getting on?' he asked.

'What are you doing here?' I asked back, trying to get my head round this chance encounter.

'Oh, just out for a run. Going to see how much of this hill I can take.'

He meant the hill we'd just coasted down for however many miles.

'It's something to do,' he said and off he went on his cool bike.

I realised it was one thing to cram a ridiculous amount of miles into a couple of weeks when you had no past form of being a cyclist and another thing entirely to be someone like James, who went out on his bike as a matter of course. I felt like joining that course in the long term and bettering myself. But I couldn't be too hard on myself at this moment in time. It was hard enough.

Just about the first building we came to in Rosemarkie was a pub and we thought it would be a poor show if we didn't pop in for a pint. They had the Happy Chappy on tap too. Two happy brothers plonked themselves down in the corner with their pints and packets of crisps. We clinked glasses. We were both grinning from ear to ear.

The two of us could easily have stayed for another, but it was best that we got to our B&B. It was a quick cycle through the village and up a hill. Our B&B looked more like a country house.

'Did you book this?' asked Stewart.

'Yep,' I said as we pedalled down the gravel path. I'd wanted us to enjoy a restful final night on the road and had booked somewhere suitably plush.

We arrived at the door and were welcomed by our host.

'You're travelling light!' said Jane.

'Oh no,' said Stewart. My brother was travelling a little too lightly. 'I've left my bag in the pub,' he said.

'You what?' I said.

'I thought that last hill was a bit too easy.'

'Stewart!'

Off he went, back through the village to retrieve his bag, while I went and had a lie down.

Thankfully my brother got his bag back and that night we walked a few hundred yards to the neighbouring village of Fortrose where we dined at The Anderson.

'Serious about food? So are we!' said the blackboard outside. The other blackboard said 'a beer drinker's mecca'. We were right in there.

The beer menu turned out to be longer than the food menu, which itself was extensive. We ordered big. This was the last night of our trip.

A group of Americans sat at the next table and we tried not to eavesdrop, but it was frankly impossible given the volume at which they were talking.

A lot of people in the north of Scotland almost seem to whisper to each other when they are out in public, whereas I've found Glaswegians – during my time in Glasgow – to be loud in comparison. These Americans though were off the scale. But at least they were having a good time.

'Yeah, Skye was wonderful,' one of them was saying.

'Beautiful,' said his wife.

'Oh really?' said one half of the other couple, who hadn't been in Skye.

'Yeah,' said the man. 'Only problem, apart from the rain, was the midgets.'

'The midgets?'

'Yeah, they ate us alive.'

My brother and I nearly choked on our pints.

'Yeah,' the man continued. 'Skye's a great place, but the problem is the midgets.'

'We haven't seen any midgets so far,' said one of the couple who hadn't been to Skye.

'Count yourself lucky, my dear.'

'How bad are they, the midgets?'

'Like mosquitos, but way worse.'

Our meals arrived and my brother and I tried to focus on the food in front of us. Fortunately the neighbouring table then moved on from midgets to some other topic.

After a fine meal, we went up to the bar and ordered one for the road. It was actually two for the road because we ordered two more beers and a pair of drams. The dram was Glenfarclas 105, one of our favourites, while the beer I ordered off the vast beer menu was a new one to me. It was called The Final Frontier and it seemed very apt.

We savoured the last of our final night in this cosy Fortrose pub then toddled off back to our country pile.

I was too excited to sleep, but thought I'd better.

The whisky helped and The Final Frontier got me there too.

Chapter 15

Boys Again

Day 15 – Rosemarkie to Hopeman

The day had come and the finish line was within reach. It was time to cycle back to Hopeman. I felt a certain nervous tension and my brother did too. I think we were excited at what lay ahead and thrilled by what we had already achieved.

We ate a vast breakfast and readied ourselves to get cracking. We'd both slept brilliantly and were full of energy.

Outside it was overcast, but not raining. It was 15 miles to Inverness and another 40 to Hopeman. Distance-wise, it was one of our shorter days and that was how I'd planned it. I didn't want the final day to be gruelling. I wanted it to be fun. This was me and my brother on bikes together for the last time until who knew when.

We left Rosemarkie, raced through Fortrose and ten minutes later we were in Avoch. I've always liked the idea of Avoch – or rather how it is said. It's pronounced 'Och'. How Scottish is that?

The tide was out and the boats in the harbour tilted in the sand. Avoch had woken up, folk out getting their newspapers and doing other messages. I liked to think that when the people of Avoch woke up they said 'och' then got on with their day.

A few miles later, we reached Munlochy Bay, where there was a bird hide. I'd never been in a bird hide before, so I popped my head in. Inside the hide was a wallchart of the birds drawn here at different times of year. Oystercatcher, redshank, mallard,

greylag goose, pink-footed goose, red-breasted merganser, cor-
morant, mute swan, whooper swan, lapwing, curlew –

'That's the fella that attacked Alasdair!' I said to my brother
who had also decided to come and hang out in the bird hide for
a bit. 'It does have a big beak.'

'You wouldn't want to be pecked by that,' agreed Stewart.

'No,' I said, and carried on checking the wallchart. Bar-tailed
godwit, wigeon, tufted duck, shelduck, common gull, herring
gull, great black-backed gull –

'Great black-backed gull! It's back!'

'It's a picture on a wall, Gary,' said my brother. 'Doesn't mean
it's here. Anyway, it's maybe not as bad as it sounds.'

'Well, Stewart, I just hope you don't get dive-bombed by a
great black-backed gull.'

'I'm wearing a helmet.'

'What about your eyes though?'

'I'll get a pair of cycling goggles, eh?'

'Do you get cycling goggles?'

'Dunno.'

We left the confined space of the bird hide for the pleasure of
cycling some more in the countryside. My brother asked me if
I'd be doing this in twenty years' time with my son.

'What, this?'

'Aye, a bike trip.'

It was a nice thought.

'Christ, I'll be sixty,' I said.

'Ha ha.'

'Here, you'll be in your late fifties!'

My brother then told me about a sixty-year-old man he knew
who still played football and was one of the fittest guys on the
team because he cycled a lot.

It was something to aim for.

In the meantime, we could now see the top of the Kessock

Bridge. It wouldn't be long before we were in Inverness again.

It was round about then the heavens opened. It really began chucking it down. Honestly, it became so wet and miserable that, when we got to the bridge, we had trouble making out Inverness on the other side – an entire city obscured from view because of the foulness of the weather. It was such a marked contrast to that sunny morning when we'd crossed the bridge with James on our way to Ullapool.

Crossing the bridge on this occasion was a nightmare. We'd just about reached the end of it when we were splashed by a lorry. The two of us got an absolute drenching and couldn't have been more wet had we gone for a dook in the firth.

Soaked and traumatised, we staggered into the Eastgate Shopping Centre and dried out in a coffee shop. We were in bad shape, when this last day was meant to be a breeze.

'Ready to go again?' I said to Stewart, finishing off my coffee.

'Not really,' sighed my brother.

We made ourselves go and forced our way out of Inverness, passing the Culloden battlefield for the second time in a week.

After a good long stint in the saddle, we arrived in Nairn. The plan was to hit one of our favourite pubs – the Bandstand Bar – for lunch and we activated that plan with relish.

The pair of us sat down, dripping wet, and ordered the soup of the day, which was fish soup. I almost fainted with a heady mixture of hunger and memory and delight as the barman brought over those steaming bowls of goodness. It smelt heavenly and it tasted just like that.

'You must be mad cycling in weather like this,' said the barman. 'I don't envy youse.'

I wanted to tell him it was fun, but he wouldn't have believed me and, right then, neither would I.

Once we'd finished our soup, we got chatting to a couple of punters at the bar. One was a local man and the other was an

Englishman up here on business. The local was telling the visitor that Nairn was the sunniest place in Britain. Not today it wasn't, but I'd heard this one before. Statistically speaking, Nairn *is* one of the sunniest places in Britain.

The Englishman found this incredible and then the local man went further and stunned him even more.

'Charlie Chaplin used to come here on his holidays,' he said.

'Really?' said the Englishman.

I nodded and joined in. 'Aye, he did.'

'Charlie Chaplin?' said my brother, looking baffled. 'Seriously?'

It was the local man's turn to nod and explain that Chaplin used to come here for some sunshine in the later years of his life in the 1970s. You couldn't beat a bit of Charlie Chaplin chat.

'John Wayne used to come here too,' said the man.

Now he was having us on, surely. But no, he was adamant. Nairn was planet Hollywood, or had been once upon a time.

'Charlie Chaplin and John Wayne in Nairn,' laughed my brother as we left the pub.

'It sounds pretty far-fetched,' I agreed. 'But remember the time David Bowie visited the Hopeman café?'

'Aye, I do,' said my brother.

Of course he did. Everyone in Hopeman knew about the day the Man Who Fell to Earth landed in Hopeman.

Bowie's son was a pupil at the time at nearby Gordonstoun. My brother had actually played in a football match against Zowie Bowie (who went on to become Duncan Jones the film director). David Bowie had spent most of the match shouting from the touchline, 'Shoot, son!' 'Tackle him!' 'Man on!'

Actually, I'm making that bit up. David Bowie wasn't at the game. But he did walk into the Hopeman café one day and order an ice cream.

'Can I have an ice cream cone?' he asked in a David Bowie voice, for it was he.

Whether he asked for a flake or not, I couldn't tell you. I'm not even sure what flavour he had. All I know is that David Bowie walked into the Hopeman café and ordered a cone – and the girl who served him didn't realise he was David Bowie. Nineteen-eighties David Bowie. *Labyrinth* David Bowie. Maybe she thought he was from Forres or something.

I wasn't there the day David Bowie walked into the Hopeman café. But I like to think that once he'd eaten his cone he played the bandit or had a game of Bubble Bobble and perhaps put one of his own songs on the jukebox. Then had a walk down Harbour Street and two old wifies came out of the post office and one of them said 'oh me, that cheel's affa thin lookin' and her friend replied 'it's thon David Bowie'.

I wish I'd been there that day David Bowie walked into the Hopeman café and ordered a cone. But at least I was there a week later when Madonna wandered in and asked for a double nougat wafer.

Cycling on a country road east of Nairn we were hit by an almost overwhelming stench of manure. This powerful assault on the nostrils nearly brought tears to my eyes. My brother looked like he was about to pass out.

We pedalled past a field with a marquee tent and saw that a wedding was underway. The couple were exchanging their vows. At least they weren't holding their noses. The tent must have been shielding them from the farmyard smells to some extent.

Passing through the tiny village of Dyke, I remarked that I'd never heard of it. My brother had.

'I used to deliver ice cream here,' said Stewart.

With him being familiar with these back roads from his happy days of ice cream deliveries, now I really did feel close to home.

The rain had stopped and by the time we were nearing Forres, I was getting really excited. I'd arranged to meet my wife and kids at the Ramnee Hotel. Clare had brought something for us – it was almost time for The Switchover.

My brother and I cycled up the hotel's gravel drive and Clare, Isabella and Alexander came out to greet us. It was so good to see them. We all had a good hug and then I looked over to the car. Strapped to the back of it were a Grifter XL and a Tuff Burner.

These would be our sets of wheels for the last 10 miles. We were going back to Hopeman as kids.

'This is going to be magic,' said Stewart.

'Let's hope so,' I said.

'I'm looking forward to seeing this,' said my wife.

'Daddy bike,' said Alexander.

In the weeks building up to our departure, I'd had a thought. How cool would it be to return to Hopeman on the Raleigh bikes of our youth?

'That way we really will leave Hopeman as grown ups and come back as kids,' I'd explained to my brother on the phone.

'Kind of like Benjamin Button?' said Stewart.

'Aye, that sort of thing.'

I'd not had much trouble tracking down a Grifter XL on the internet. I'd figured there would be someone out there trying to sell the very bike I craved. I paid a hundred quid to a bloke in Hertfordshire and the bike arrived in a box a couple of days later.

What was remarkable though was my brother's Tuff Burner. He hadn't bought it over the internet or anywhere else. He'd taken it out of the garage. Stewart's Tuff Burner was the Tuff Burner he'd ridden as a child. It had been hanging up in the garage for the best part of thirty years.

'Are you sure you'll be able to ride that thing?' I'd asked on the phone.

'It doesn't look too bad,' he'd said. 'It's a bit dusty. There's a guy at my work who's into fixing bikes. I'll get him to take a look at it.'

His friend with the skills and the tools had done a great job on it. By the time he was finished with it, Stewart's Tuff Burner looked brand new.

I was still struggling to get my head round it, even now, as he lifted it off the back of the car. I couldn't believe he still had it – and that he was about to get on it.

'Are you sure you'll get to Hopeman on these bikes?' Clare asked.

It was a fair enough question.

'Ach, we'll be fine,' I said. 'Won't we, Stewart?'

'Think so.'

Before we set off, we had a quick coffee in the hotel. This place meant a lot to my wife and me. We'd held our wedding reception here. My brother, naturally, had been my best man.

Sitting here all these years later, with my daughter on my knee and my son running around, life was so different now, and better too. It was so good to see my family again. Not seeing them for so long had been tough. I don't know how Dad had coped being away at sea for up to a month at a time.

'Right,' I said, finishing my coffee. 'Let's hit the road.'

I'd see the kids again in an hour's time, or however long it took me to cycle from Forres to Hopeman on a Grifter XL.

We tied the Green Lantern and the White Knight to the back of the car. They'd served us well these past two weeks. Not a single puncture between us either, which was just as well since neither of us was entirely sure how to deal with a puncture. Really, on the basis of our preparation, we hardly deserved to have made it this far.

'Okay, Stewart,' I said, getting on my Grifter XL, which felt tiny.

'Sure,' said Stewart, jumping on his Tuff Burner and looking like a giant.

We were both smiling. I was ten again and he was eight.

Clare set off back to Hopeman with the kids and left us to it.

Stewart immediately started doing wheelies.

'Show off,' I said.

I could barely lift the front wheel of my Grifter XL as a child and it was still something of a task now. Also the handlebars were a bit wobbly. I couldn't have tightened them properly. Hmm. I didn't want my handlebars coming off between here and Hopeman. I left the wheelies alone and just focused on pedalling the thing.

Having ridden an adult bike for the past fortnight – a giant hybrid one at that – it felt odd sitting so close to the ground and that was with the seat right up. My knees, though right as rain, seemed awfully high. I also kept changing gear without even meaning to, forgetting that the right grip was the gear shift. This Grifter XL business was taking some getting used to. The seat was comfy though, comfier than I remembered it being. I'd have said it was as comfy as the seat on the Green Lantern.

As we left Forres, my seat started wobbling. It wasn't secure either. Between that and the swivelling handlebars, I felt like I was on a clown's bicycle. All I needed was a horn. The Grifter XL experience wasn't panning out as I'd imagined it. Typically, I hadn't really practised on it. As with everything else, I'd assumed it would all be fine.

This was hard work and possibly dangerous. The bike wasn't roadworthy.

Everything changed when I decided not to sit down any more and discovered it was easier to pedal standing up. That was more like it. I was able to get a better purchase on the pedals and the seat wasn't swivelling around any more because I wasn't sitting on it. I just had to be careful with the handlebars.

I began to build up some speed and started to get a hang of the gears – how fun to have that twisting motion again. I was getting all nostalgic except I was actually living it. Currently I was in the highest of my three gears and was fairly eating up the road to Kinloss.

'Hey, slow down!' cried Stewart, who was trailing in my wake. I'd forgotten he was on an even smaller and gearless Tuff Burner. So I slowed down a bit. I glanced down and saw the flash of neon that was the Grifter XL logo on the crossbar and smiled at the sight of my red front mudguard. What a machine – and I was cycling back to Hopeman on it. We'd be on Dunbar Street before long.

Ahead of the trip, I'd asked various friends about the bikes they'd had as kids and it had become abundantly clear that everyone loved talking about the bikes of their youth.

Keith talked about his Grifter and how he'd almost drowned riding it off the end of the pier.

Michael's Raleigh Outlander got nicked, but he found it 'buried under 15,000 cigarettes'. I wished I'd found my Strika under a pile of fags.

Dave had a Raleigh Arena, 'a five-speed racer that took me places, though I always wanted a Grifter'.

Ally, like me, had a Grifter XL, which he described as 'a road roller'.

Alex had a Raleigh Banana which he rode wearing a matching cycling top – 'lightning!'

Brian had a Raleigh Night Burner – 'team black and red with matching Skyway wheel at the front, rad!'

Denis had a Raleigh Diamondback with a back-pedal brake.

Martin had a blue and white BMX that his granny picked up on holiday in Jersey and took back on the plane. 'I remember her, aged seventy-five, wheeling it through customs.'

My other friend Martin had a Grifter that he was forever trying to destroy, so that he might get a BMX. 'The Grifter always won,' he said.

Then there was Scott, who had the most futuristic bike of them all, the Raleigh Vektar, which had its own crazy control panel with speedometer and spacy sound effects.

My brother remembered Scott and him finding the biggest brae around so Scott could tear down it on his Vektar while checking his velocity. He must have been trying to achieve warp speed.

Scott's still with us – he didn't go back to the future.

Meanwhile, here were me and my brother going forward to go back on our bikes of old. I looked over my shoulder at Stewart on his blue and yellow dream machine. Scott, the Vektar owner, had said my brother's Tuff Burner 'was the boy'. I found it hard to disagree with him. That bike hadn't lost any of its cool, even though Stewart looked like he had outgrown it. He was doing a fine job though. It looked like we might make Hopeman yet.

We came to the humpback bridge at Roseisle, which brought back happy memories for us. How many times had we gone over that bridge in the family car, Mam and Dad telling us to 'hold on to your bellies!' before we felt that funny sensation in our stomachs as the car dipped over the bridge.

As we went over it now on a Tuff Burner and a Grifter XL, my brother and I shouted: 'Hold on to your belly!'

Just after that, I noticed some broken glass on the road and narrowly managed to avoid it. I didn't want to be suffering a puncture at this late stage, a couple of miles from home.

'Glass!' I called out to Stewart behind me.

'It's okay, it's a Tuff Burner,' he said, implying that the blue wheels on his bike were somehow glass-proof. He either managed to miss the glass or those brightly coloured wheels actually were invincible.

As we cycled through the tiny village of College of Roseisle we passed a woman walking with her wee boy who was riding a BMX. He looked about the same age as I was when I'd last ridden a Grifter XL. I bet he loved that bike of his.

Then we came to the big hill known locally as the Seven Towers. It was the only hill of real note between Forres and Hopeman and the question was: were we going to make it up it on a Grifter XL and a Tuff Burner?

Standing up, I picked my gear and pedalled for all I was worth. Stewart put in an extra huge effort too and we both made it to the top.

'That was fun!' I said.

'Aye,' said Stewart. 'It wasn't so much fun for Dad, this hill, was it?'

I laughed. When Dad was a boy he'd gone down this hill on his bike and realised only too late that his brakes weren't working. He'd gone right off the road at the bottom and ended up in the field.

A few minutes later, we caught our first glimpse of Hopeman. The harbour was a sight for sore eyes. I'd been looking forward to this moment and now that it was here I was almost overwhelmed by it.

We cycled into Hopeman and, when we got to the second of the village's two bus stops, we cut down the lane. This was it … at the end of this lane was Dunbar Street.

We could see our family and friends waiting for us and they'd just seen us and were waving.

'Watch the bollard!' I said to Stewart as we neared the scene of the salad cream sandwich incident.

'I'm watching it,' he said, as he cycled round it on his Tuff Burner.

Incredible. My brother was back in one piece.

We must have looked ridiculous in the eyes of our welcome party, but we must also have looked pretty happy. The faces of our pals and relatives seemed to show that they were happy – and perhaps relieved too.

The only thing that could have topped this return from our 1,000-mile bike ride round the country would have been the sight of my silver Strika at the back gate. But I had my Grifter XL and my brother and the rest of my family.

It was good to be home.

Some six months later, on a crisp and clear Christmas morning, I took my son out on the tiny new bike he'd got from Santa. Santa could have given Alexander any colour of bike, but in the end he'd delivered a silver one.